Lesson plans:
Sarah Donnelly
Nick Duncan

Controlled assessment:
Nick Duncan
Jane Hingley
Stuart Sage

EAL support:
Simon Murison-Bowie
Dianne Excell

WJEC GCSE English and English Language

Higher

Teacher Guide

www.pearsonschools.co.uk

✓ Free online support
✓ Useful weblinks
✓ 24 hour online ordering

0845 630 22 22

naldic

EAL
in partnership with the National Association for Language Development in the Curriculum

Heinemann
Part of Pearson

Heinemann is an imprint of Pearson Education Limited, a company incorporated in England and Wales, having its registered office at Edinburgh Gate, Harlow, Essex, CM20 2JE. Registered company number: 872828

www.pearsonschoolsandfecolleges.co.uk

Heinemann is the registered trademark of Pearson Education Limited

Text © Pearson Education Limited 2010

EAL introduction and EAL lesson plan content © NALDIC

First published 2010

14 13 12 11 10
10 9 8 7 6 5 4 3 2

British Library Cataloguing in Publication Data
A catalogue record for this book is available from the British Library on request.

ISBN 978 0 435 01689 0

Designed and produced by Kamae Design, Oxford
Cover design by Wooden Ark Studios, Leeds
Picture research by Sally Cole
Cover photo © Gaertner/Alamy
Printed in the UK by Ashford Colour Press

Acknowledgements
We would like to thank the schools, who were involved in this project, for their invaluable help creating exam answers for this book.

The author and publisher would like to thank the following individuals and organisations for permission to reproduce photographs:
p32©Klaus Tiedge/Corbis

Every effort has been made to contact copyright holders of material reproduced in this book. Any omissions will be rectified in subsequent printings if notice is given to the publishers.
Worksheet 1.1: 'Help! It's the scare Bear bunch' by Peter Baumgartner from *The Daily Telegraph* Magazine, 27th January, 2001. Used by permission of the Telegraph Media Group Limited; **Worksheets 1.27 and 1.53**: WWF Leaflet in support of Tigers, 'What will you do when I'm gone?' Produced by the WWF. Used with permission; **Worksheet 1.39**: Leaflet from Alzheimer's Research Trust, 'Without immediate funding, vital Alzheimer's research will come to a halt.' Published by the Alzheimer's Research Trust used with permission; **Worksheet 1.47**: 'Please will you stop paying to have my people murdered?' campaign advertisement from *Friends of the Earth*. Used with permission; **Worksheet 2.27**: Transcript of Tony Blair speech. Reproduced by permission of the BBC; **Worksheet 4.1**: 'Unrelated Incidents – No 3' by Tom Leonard © Tom Leonard from *Outside the narrative* (Poems 1965–2009), published by Etruscan Books/WorldPower 2009; **Worksheet 4.8**: Transcript: *Word on the Street* as broadcast by the BBC on 24 August 2005. Reproduced by permission of the BBC; **Worksheet 4.14**: 'Inter Group GCSE English – Speaking and Listening Training and Guidance'. Reproduced by permission of WJEC.

Contents

Introduction 4

Functional Skills matching chart 6

GradeStudio 9

NALDIC guidance for teaching EAL students 12

Suggested teaching sequence, sample strategies and activities for EAL development 16

NALDIC glossary of EAL teaching and learning techniques 19

Unit 1: Reading non-fiction texts 24

1.1 Locating and retrieving information 24

1.2 Impressions 36

1.3 Viewpoint and attitude 40

1.4 Intended audience 44

1.5 Analysis of persuasive techniques 48

1.6 Comparison and evaluation of texts 68

Unit 2: Writing information and ideas 72

2.1 Informal letters 72

2.2 Formal letters 74

2.3 Reports 76

2.4 Articles 80

2.5 Leaflets 84

2.6 Speeches/talks 86

2.7 Reviews 90

Unit 4: Studying spoken language 92

4.1 Capturing spoken language 92

4.2 Language change, choice and variation 98

Controlled assessment guidance 104

Study of spoken language 104

Literary reading 112

Open writing 120

Mark scheme for sample Reading and Writing papers 132

Introduction

WJEC English and English Language Higher resources from Heinemann

The endorsed WJEC English and English Language resources from Heinemann support the WJEC GCSE English and WJEC GCSE English Language specifications.

GCSE English

	Student Book	Teacher Guide
Unit 1 Reading: non-fiction texts	✓	✓
Unit 2: Writing: information and ideas	✓	✓
Unit 3: Reading and Writing (Controlled Assessment)		✓
Unit 4: Speaking and Listening (Controlled Assessment)	✓	✓

GCSE English Language

	Student Book	Teacher Guide
Unit 1 Reading: non fiction texts	✓	✓
Unit 2: Writing: information and ideas	✓	✓
Unit 3: Studying written language and Using language (Controlled assessment)		✓
Unit 4: Studying spoken language (Controlled assessment)	✓	✓

How do the English and English Language resources work?

The WJEC GCSE English and English Language Higher Teacher Guide and WJEC GCSE English and English Language Higher ActiveTeach are explicitly linked to the WJEC GCSE English and English Language Higher Student Book.

All of the resources are divided into four units which directly match the WJEC specifications and link seamlessly together. Unit 4 in the Student Book outlines the skills needed for the spoken language controlled assessment element of the specification. This, as with Units 1 and 2, is further supported by lesson plans and guidance in the Teacher Guide.

Differentiation

The Student Book and lesson plans have been written with the precise needs of your Higher Tier students in mind, providing specific advice, activities and sample answers to enable them to get the best results. The reading and writing controlled assessment guidance is not tiered. Foundation Tier material is also available, so you can be confident that all your students are supported.

EAL advice

Each step-by-step visual lesson plan incorporates specific EAL advice in partnership with the National Association for Language Development in the Curriculum.

How do the resources work together?

The Student Book outlines the teaching and learning requirements of the specification. GradeStudio provides graded sample answers, examiner comments and advice so students can get the best results. Most lessons also include peer/self-assessment and advice about moving up the grades.

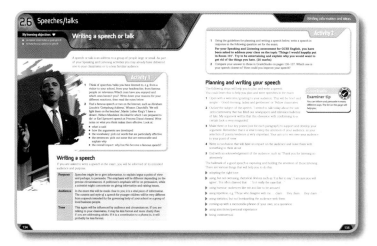

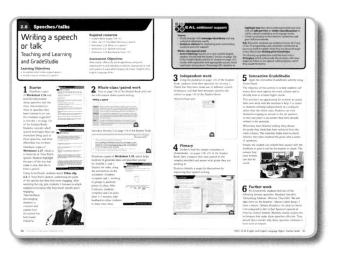

The Teacher Guide supports the teaching lessons with planning guidance and delivery ideas including worksheets for each lesson. In addition, there is controlled assessment guidance for Units 3 and 4. The lesson plans are easy to follow and include starters and plenaries, advice about how to carry out the Student Book activities (including suggested answers to save you time) plus guidance on how to incorporate the additional ActiveTeach assets into your lessons.

The ActiveTeach CD-ROM includes BBC footage to help motivate students, plus interactive GradeStudio activities to help students get to grips with the grading criteria. ActiveTeach functionality has been designed for whole-class teaching and enables you to zoom in on extracts and annotate using the whiteboard. See pages 8–11 for more tips about using the ActiveTeach CD-ROM and GradeStudio activities in the classroom.

Functional Skills matching chart

Functional Skills in English are the skills that we use to communicate everyday: reading, writing, and speaking and listening.

Functional Skills can be taught alongside the existing programmes of study in Key Stages 3 and 4. Many students may be ready to master Level 1 when in Year 9 or even lower down in school, while other students may take Level 1 or 2 assessments in Key Stage 4 in order to attain points worth half a GCSE. Functional Skills can also be taught as separate components or skills.

Below are three grids (Reading, Speaking, Listening and Communication, and Writing) that list the Functional Skills standards and link them to the WJEC specification to help you embed Functional Skills into your teaching. A commentary has been added to help you to interpret the standards.

Also available is a Student Book and Teacher Guide tailored to the WJEC Functional English qualification. The WJEC Functional English Student Book and the accompanying Teacher Guide have been designed to support teachers to help students achieve Level 2 in the WJEC Functional Skills English qualification.

Level 2 Functional Skills Reading standard: Select, read, understand and compare texts and use them to gather information, ideas, arguments and opinions.

QCDA Criteria for Level 2 Functional Skills	Links to Assessment Objectives for GCSE English and GCSE English Language	Commentary
Select and use different types of texts to obtain and utilise relevant information.	Read and understand texts, selecting material appropriate to purpose, collating from different sources and making comparisons and cross-references as appropriate.	The aim here is to ensure that students are able to understand a wide range of different texts and resources, find information and explain what they have found out. The key word for obtaining information is *relevant*.
Read and summarise succinctly, information/ideas from different sources.	Read and understand texts, selecting material appropriate to purpose, collating from different sources and making comparisons and cross-references as appropriate.	The specific skill being used for Functional Skills is the ability to read and summarise information. Students need to practise reading texts and condensing the information so that it still makes sense but is much shorter (while making sure the meaning stays the same as the original text). It is important that relevant information is carefully selected.
Identify the purposes of texts and comment on how meaning is conveyed.	Develop and sustain interpretations of writers' ideas and perspectives.	Students need to understand what the writer is trying to do or achieve and understand that techniques may be used to persuade the reader to think or feel a certain way.
Detect point of view, implicit meaning and/ or bias.	Explain and evaluate how writers use linguistic, grammatical, structural and presentational features to achieve effects and engage and influence the reader.	This Functional Skills standard is simpler than the GCSE requirement as there is no need to assess the text. However, it is essential that students are taught how to detect and understand a point of view. They may also need to look for bias.

Analyse texts in relation to audience needs and consider suitable responses.	Read and understand texts, selecting material appropriate to purpose, collating from different sources and making comparisons and cross-references as appropriate.	Students will need to read texts in detail and then produce a response based on what they have read and the audience they are writing for. Students must base their answers only on the texts they have read, and not on prior knowledge.

Level 2 Functional Skills Speaking, listening and communication standard: Make a range of contributions to discussions in a range of contexts, including those that are unfamiliar, and make effective presentations.

QCDA Criteria for Level 2 Functional Skills	Links to Assessment objectives for GCSE English and GCSE English Language	Commentary
Consider complex information and give a relevant, cogent response in appropriate language.	Listen and respond to speakers' ideas, perspectives and how they construct and express their meanings.	Level 2 students must be able to listen to a range of information, take on board what they have heard and use the information as a basis for their own response. They must be able to judge the tone and situation in which they are given information so they are able to respond using the correct tone and language themselves.
Present information and ideas clearly and persuasively to others.	Speak to communicate clearly and purposefully; structure and sustain talk, adapting it to different situations and audiences; use standard English and a variety of techniques as appropriate.	At Level 2, all communication must be clear. The ability to communicate persuasively is essential to help an audience to remain focused on what they are saying.
Adapt contributions to suit audience, purpose and situation.	Speak to communicate clearly and purposefully; structure and sustain talk, adapting it to different situations and audiences; use standard English and a variety of techniques as appropriate.	Successful Level 2 students are able to listen to other people's views and adapt their own ideas to suit what they have heard. The ability to be flexible in a discussion is crucial and any changes or adaptations they make during a presentation must take into account the audience and the way it has responded to both the student and the other speakers.
Make significant contributions to discussions, taking a range of roles and helping to move discussion forward.	Interact with others, shaping meanings through suggestions, comments and questions and drawing ideas together.	'Significant contributions' simply means that candidates have to include plenty of detail and must play a key role in group situations or have an extended role. Unfortunately, this is where many students cause concern because they do not develop their ideas and talk in sufficient detail. They are required to take on different roles (such as being the leader of a group or the chair of a discussion, or considering a different view to that which they normally hold) and must continually move the discussion and their ideas forward towards a conclusion. This might involve asking questions, summarising views or giving an overall final decision.

Level 2 Functional Skills Writing standard: Write a range of texts, including extended written documents, communicating information, ideas and opinions, effectively and persuasively.

QCDA Criteria for Level 2 Functional Skills	Links to Assessment Objectives for GCSE English and GCSE English Language	Commentary
Present information/ideas concisely, logically and persuasively.	Organise information and ideas into structured and sequenced sentences, paragraphs and whole texts, using a variety of linguistic and structural features to support cohesion and overall coherence.	Students must begin with a clear plan of what to write. They will receive no credit for planning, so should keep it short, but it will ensure they remain organised and focused when writing. They must learn and use persuasive techniques when appropriate.
Present information on complex subjects clearly and concisely.	Organise information and ideas into structured and sequenced sentences, paragraphs and whole texts, using a variety of linguistic and structural features to support cohesion and overall coherence.	Students may be asked to write on complex subjects. They may be given some guidance or stimulus: the key to success is developing these and adding their own ideas. Often writing topics will be open to a number of different interpretations; what matters is to make sure they give the reader the information in a clear way.
Use a range of writing styles for different purposes.	Write clearly, effectively and imaginatively, using and adapting forms and selecting vocabulary appropriate to task and purpose in ways which engage the reader.	Students will always be told which format to use in a response. Their job is to read the task closely in order to fully understand the *purpose* of their writing. They might be asked to persuade, argue, advise or entertain a reader and need to adapt language, style and content to fit this purpose. The range of skills they can demonstrate will of course contribute to their overall success but making their work suitable for the reader and clear is of utmost importance.
Use a range of sentence structures, including complex sentences, and paragraphs to organise written work effectively.	Use a range of sentence structures for clarity, purpose and effect, with accurate punctuation and spelling.	Level 2 writing must be varied so it is interesting, engaging and clear for the reader. Students need to think about using a range of sentence lengths and types to give their work variety and interest.
Punctuate written text using commas, apostrophes and inverted commas accurately.	Use a range of sentence structures for clarity, purpose and effect, with accurate punctuation and spelling.	There is no need to create deliberate effect with punctuation for a Level 2 pass mark. The key here is that most punctuation needs to be accurate to achieve Level 2 writing and candidates need to work consciously to ensure their work is not only clear in terms of sense but also in terms of punctuation. Varying punctuation where appropriate to demonstrate to the examiner a range of skills also receives credit. Punctuation, spelling and grammar are together worth 45% of the final mark for writing.
Ensure written work is fit for purpose and audience, with accurate spelling and grammar that support clear meaning in a range of text types.	Use a range of sentence structures for clarity, purpose and effect, with accurate punctuation and spelling.	Spellings should be accurate in Level 2 writing, particularly those words that are functional and used in everyday writing. Students can make some errors with complex and extended vocabulary, but these should be kept to a minimum. Level 2 writers also need to check the tenses are accurate in written work.

GradeStudio

GradeStudio is a unique resource designed to help students achieve their best with sample questions, graded answers and examiner tips. GradeStudio has been designed to help improve students' answers to exam questions and ultimately their grades.

GradeStudio features throughout the Student Book with extensive examiner guidance and opportunities for students to reflect on and improve their learning. In addition to this interactive GradeStudio can be found on the ActiveTeach CD-ROM. These interactive activities build on the GradeStudio material in the Student Book and are ideal for whole-class teaching.

The main features of GradeStudio include:

- A **real examiner** helps you to guide your students through sample answers, mark schemes and helps them assess their own and their peers' work.
- An easy to use **Slider** helps students to understand the mark scheme and grade requirements.
- The activities have been written specifically for higher or foundation students. Every question has sample answers for relevant grades so these activities are suitable for **students of both tiers**.
- Each activity and sample answer can be printed out to aid preparation and to be used as you work through the activities front of class.

There are four types of interactive GradeStudio activity:

1 Write a sample answer and self assess

Learning objective:

- To help students self-assess their work against the mark scheme and identify how to achieve higher marks

This activity is an opportunity for students to assess their own work with the examiner's help. Students can time themselves typing an answer to the set question. Or they can paste in an answer they have already written to the question. When they have finished writing, they choose the grade they think they have achieved from the mark scheme. The examiner helps them to check whether they have reached this grade with a series of questions. Finally, the student can rework their answer with the feedback or print it out for the teacher to check. The answer they have written can also be saved.

1 Students are asked if they want to time themselves answering the question. Alternatively they can skip this and paste an answer they have already written to this question.

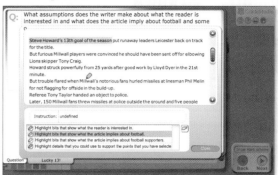

2 Students can analyse the question and highlight relevant details.

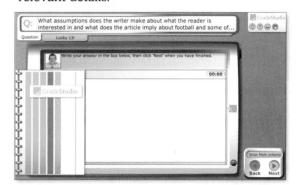

3 Students type/paste their answer in the space provided and select which grade they think it has achieved.

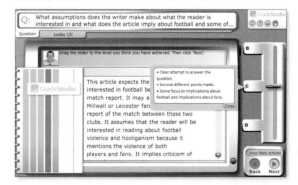

4 Students are prompted to highlight where they have met criteria of the mark scheme and/or answer multiple-choice questions.

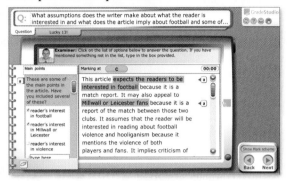

5 Students can then compare their answer with an answer written by the examiner at that grade for further self-assessment opportunities.

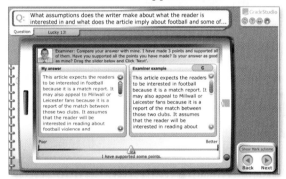

2 Comparing a sample answer

Learning objectives:
- To understand what skills are required at different grades
- To understand that there are different ways to achieve the same grade

This activity gives a range of sample answers for each grade.

Students analyse and compare answers to the same grade and at different grades. Each answer has examiner comments so that students can understand what skills are required at each grade and see that there are different ways to achieve the same grade.

Students will become familiar with the criteria specific to each grade. Students will also be shown the best way to arrive at that grade. In addition by comparing answers to the same question students can see how questions are commonly misinterpreted and marks are lost.

1 Initially students can analyse the question and highlight relevant details.

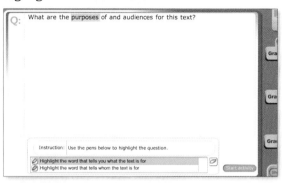

2 A grade is chosen by moving the slider to the right of the screen to show sample answers at that grade.

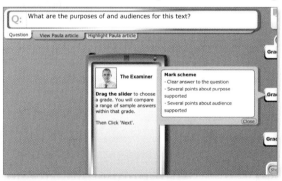

3 The class is presented with different ways of achieving the selected grade. They compare the sample answers by highlighting where they think the marks have been awarded in each sample.

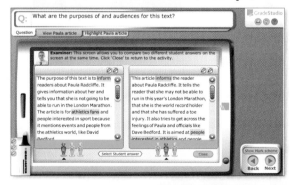

4 Finally the class matches the samples answers to the examiner comments, to check they have understood where the marks have been allocated or lost.

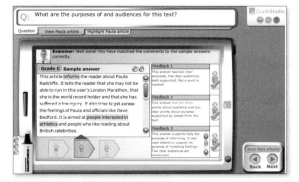

3 Improving a sample answer

Learning objective:
- To show how to move answers up a grade

This activity is an excellent way to show students, of all abilities, how to improve answers to achieve the next grade. The teacher selects a grade. The class will suggest improvements to the sample answer which can be typed on to your whiteboard. The printout for this activity allows the student to write down their own improvements in the classroom or at home.

You can then see how the examiner would improve the answer and compare the suggestions to those made by the class.

1 Initially students can analyse the question and highlight relevant details.

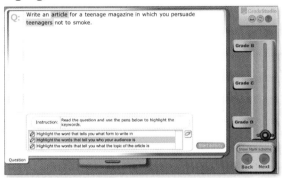

2 The teacher annotates and discusses how to improve the sample answer with the class. The examiner will then reveal his or her suggestions and the class can discuss why this improved the grade.

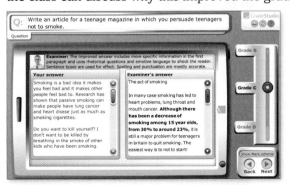

3 The mark scheme can be revealed at any time

4 Mark a sample answer

Learning objective:
- To understand the mark scheme

This activity will help you and your students pull apart a sample answer with a highlighting tool. Your students will then assess the strengths and weaknesses of each section by answering a series of questions. At the end of their analysis the students can suggest the grade of the sample answer.

This activity gives the students a chance to be the examiner and really understand how the questions are marked.

1 Initially students can analyse the question and highlight relevant details.

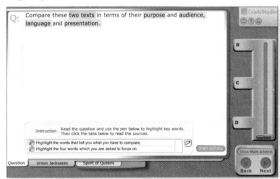

2 Students highlight parts of the sample answer when prompted by the examiner. Based on this analysis students decide the grade the answer deserves, which is checked by the examiner.

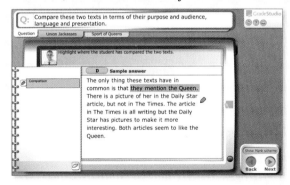

NALDIC guidance for teaching EAL students

Introduction

A growing number of schools and teachers are now supporting students with English as an Additional Language (EAL). More than one in ten secondary students is, or is becoming, bilingual and over 240 languages are spoken by students in UK schools, the most widely used being Panjabi, Urdu, Bengali, Gujarati, Somali, Polish, Arabic, Portuguese, Turkish and Tamil. This Teacher Guide is designed to help your lesson delivery and to give suggestions on how to differentiate materials for your students.

Students learning EAL will vary in their proficiency in their first language *and* in their proficiency in English. Some, but not all, will be fluent in their first language and have age-appropriate academic literacy skills in that language. Some will have age-appropriate skills in English similar to their peers. Others will be at very early stages. Others may be fluent in certain uses of English, but have less secure skills in other areas, for example written academic English. Similarly, students will use their first language skills for different purposes at different times.

For the purposes of this guide, three terms are used to describe students' English language levels:

- *new* to English language and literacy (likely to be new to the UK and unable to successfully participate in curriculum studies without further assistance and support)
- *exploring* English language and literacy (likely to be able to communicate in everyday and some written English. They may have arrived in the UK during KS3 and their English is likely to show shortfalls in relation to both academic and social activities)
- *consolidating* English language and literacy (likely to be competent in spoken English in the classroom and in informal situations but this fluency may not be reflected in academic reading and writing). (RBKC, 2006)

Attainment for all of these students is likely to vary significantly between speaking and listening, reading and writing, but they often make faster progress than English-speaking peers assessed at the same levels in National Curriculum English.

Broad principles

When faced with the linguistic challenges of a multilingual classroom, you will need to take a broad view of the language development of EAL students. It's not just about developing students' knowledge of bits of English vocabulary and grammar, nor of teaching these through 'extra' activities. EAL students will be learning about English as a subject at the same time as they are learning about and through English as a language. They will also be at different stages in this process. Learning a new language requires time, exposure and opportunities to understand meanings through interaction and independent reflection.

Context

Language does not occur in a vacuum, but in a context, and this context affects the way things are written and said. First of all, there is the 'context of culture', where users share common assumptions in relation to the way things are done, whether this is buying some bread or delivering a physics lesson. Secondly, language is used within a 'context of situation'. This means the language used varies according to the relationship of those involved, from speaker to speaker, from topic to topic, according to purpose and situation.

All speakers are instinctively aware of these differences in their first languages. There are also variations in language according to social class, region and ethnic group. In schools, language also varies from subject to subject. For example, the language used in Maths is very different from that used in English or History. EAL learners need to become familiar with the variations in written and spoken language that are used in subjects, schools and local communities, as well as understanding the cultural expectations, beliefs and practices associated with the language.

Communication

Language is essentially a means of communication. We use language to interact with one another and to express our feelings or viewpoints, our needs and to learn about the world. The functional nature of language in the classroom means an EAL student cannot focus

solely on the mastery of grammar or the understanding of vocabulary. Research indicates that language learning is most effective when learners are involved in meaningful situations. Learners acquire language through social interaction but also through activities that offer intellectual challenge.

> Aim to give learners the opportunity to engage in social interaction while undertaking activities that offer cognitive challenge. Just as students are marked on the content of their work, EAL students also need to receive feedback on their language use.

Another key principle is the interdependence of speaking, listening, reading and writing. These are often presented as 'four' skills, but in real-life contexts they are naturally interdependent. In real life, students acquire the ability to use them simultaneously and interdependently. Their language processes develop as they use multimodal technologies such as film, video and ICT.

> You will need to provide EAL learners with opportunities to develop their language abilities in ways which recognise the interdependence of speaking, listening, reading and writing.

Language learning is not short term. It takes place over time and individual learners acquire language at different rates. There are many contributing factors, such as linguistic or educational backgrounds. Learners' thinking and learning styles, motivation and personality also play a role. You may have seen that EAL learners frequently acquire informal conversational skills more quickly than academic language skills (which may take five to seven years to develop). In order to plan appropriately for the linguistically diverse classroom, it is essential to understand the progression of language from spoken (e.g. playground talk) through to written (e.g. exploratory talk).

It is widely acknowledged that bilingualism is an asset and enhances learners' linguistic and cognitive skills. However, in order for students to benefit fully they need to be very proficient in both languages. This implies that the most effective school environment for EAL learners is one in which the development of the first language for both academic and social purposes is promoted alongside the learning of English. EAL learners who are literate in their first language have many advantages. Literacy in another language helps them to make sense of academic texts in English as they have an understanding of how different kinds of texts work.

Importantly, learning a new language also offers them insights into their first languages.

Implications for teaching and learning

The principles above have many implications when it comes to planning for and teaching your students. They underpin many aspects of successful teaching in linguistically diverse classrooms, such as:
- making the most of a student's prior knowledge and understanding in their first language and English
- encouraging learners to seek meaning through communicative and independent activities
- helping a student to understand source materials and supporting them to reflect their understanding in their own writing in English
- paying attention to culturally and contextually specific ways of using language
- activities which focus on specific aspects of English at word, sentence and text level which EAL students may find more difficult.

Some detailed practical suggestions are given in the table on the next page.

Rationale for suggested approaches

Reading: Structuring texts

The conventional ways of selecting and structuring information, presenting it in specific formats for different purposes and expressing it with specific features of language, often seem 'natural' to fluent and experienced first-language users of English. Students have had many years of exposure to these ways of using language at home and at school before they reach your classroom.

EAL students with limited exposure to different types of text in English are at a disadvantage, especially if the practices in their first language are quite different.

Reading: Reading for meaning

Many EAL learners will also be at a disadvantage when trying to interpret clues to predict meanings in texts. This may be because the text describes something which is beyond their current experience.

It is important to remember that most bilingual learners will have been exposed to a range of learning and literacy practices before they come into a UK school. The challenge is to build on these experiences pragmatically.

EAL insights	Practical implications
Different cultures and languages use different ways of expressing meaning, not just different vocabulary and grammar.	• Make the socio-cultural assumptions in your talk, tasks and materials explicit. • Give students opportunities to reflect on differences and similarities.
EAL learners need to be able to adapt spoken and written language to suit the context. They also need to use spoken or written language in accepted and predictable ways to perform particular purposes and to communicate meaning.	• Give students a variety of opportunities to engage in understanding in ways which are appropriate to the subject. • Provide feedback on students' language use.
EAL learners may have strengths and weaknesses within the skill sets of speaking and listening, reading and writing.	• Be sensitive to the different skills profiles of learners and the interdependence of speaking, listening, reading and writing. • Groupings based on attainment in reading or writing may not always be appropriate. • EAL learners will benefit from an additional focus on speaking and listening activities as a bridge to reading and writing.
EAL learners will not necessarily acquire English skills in the same order as first language speakers.	• Include strategies which build on students' strengths, for example in spoken English or from their first language. • Where more than one student shares a language, opportunities for discussion in that language should be encouraged, as should developing independent translation skills.
EAL learners will be acquiring English language skills across the curriculum and will also be using these skills across the curriculum.	• Work to develop learners' oral language skills alongside their literacy skills. • Build on learners' prior knowledge and the resources they bring. • Make links with students' other languages and work across the curriculum to build their language and literacy capacity.
Bilingualism and bi-culturalism are assets and can enhance learners' linguistic and cognitive skills.	• Build in opportunities to promote the use of first languages for academic and social purposes.

Reading: Going beyond the text

Of course, fluent users of English in your classroom do not simply follow a text to recover meaning from the words and sentences: they have to know how to make use of the information for different purposes. This ability to go beyond the text cannot be taught through just the 'nuts and bolts' of language itself: it has to be supported by increasing familiarity with culturally established ways of seeing, knowing and understanding.

EAL learners with a limited experience of dealing with written texts in English may find this aspect of reading an invisible but constant problem. Similarly, the task of acquiring new vocabulary is not a simple one to be solved by exposing students to 'key words'. Words have multiple meanings and are used with different emphases in different contexts and students need continued exposure to these meanings.

Writing

Most writing tasks are developed from the curriculum and EAL students may not fully understand the curriculum meanings expressed through spoken English. Words change their meaning according to the context, and the classroom is full of metaphorical and figurative uses of language which are open to misunderstandings. This lack of understanding of content meaning often causes major difficulties in selecting and including appropriate information in writing tasks.

Cameron (2003) identifies some of the following problems that KS4/post-16 EAL students have in writing:

1 Even high level (or **consolidating**) EAL learners have difficulty in using ideas from source materials in their own writing.

2 **Consolidating** EAL learners may also have difficulty in judging nuances of style, and still experience some of the same problems as their less proficient EAL

peers (**new** and **exploring**) with the use of articles, choice of the correct preposition in fixed phrases, and subject–verb agreement.

3 'Delexical' verbs, i.e. verbs that are 'so frequently used and in so many different contexts that the link between the verb and its meaning becomes quite weak', such as 'put', 'do', 'have', 'make' or 'go'. Examples include sentences such as 'make a stop to this', instead of 'put a stop to', and 'they will do more fun' instead of 'they will have more fun'.

4 Difficulties with sentence grammar related to the length of clause constituents and use of adverbials and subordination to develop more complex sentence structure.

Although some of these common areas of difficulty may benefit from specific teaching, Gibbons (2002) likens word- and sentence-level work to focusing a pair of binoculars. Your first gaze is the whole vista and after a while you use the binoculars to hone in on a detail of the landscape. You know how to locate this detail because you have already seen it as part of the whole. When you have finished focusing on the detail, you will probably return to the whole panorama again but with an enhanced sense of what is there. Additional word- and sentence-level activities need to be compatible with this 'whole vista' approach and provide further opportunities for 'message abundancy' (see Gibbons' explanation under 'Practical application' below).

Linking reading, writing, speaking and listening

Learning to write in EAL is inextricably linked to learning English and curriculum content through spoken English at the same time. Given that spoken English is not necessarily the same as the written form, it is important to pay attention to bilingual students' writing in English, even when they seem to understand spoken communication reasonably well.

> This suggests that reading and writing tasks should start with and be supported by teaching and group activities which use spoken English in conjunction with relevant visual materials, realia and hands-on experiential learning tasks. This will go a long way to making meanings comprehensible.

Practical application

Gibbons (2008) describes what this might look like in practical terms:

> 'If you were a second language learner in that class, you would have had opportunities for participating in an initial shared experience, which is watching the video with everybody else; hearing everyday language alongside academic language in the interactions between teachers and students – the Janus-like talk;

seeing the key points written on the board, so you have got a visual representation of what you're hearing; having the difference between everyday and technical language highlighted through the colour-coding; having access to a chart of definitions; getting practice in putting new concepts into practice; and, finally, using the learning in a new context.'

Gibbons has used the term 'message abundancy' to describe this sort of teaching sequence – 'So that you have more than one bite of the apple, you don't just get told one thing once':

> 'A lot of EAL students that I've interviewed in secondary say their teachers talk too quickly. I don't think it's actually the speed of the talk that they're responding to, I think it's the speed at which information is given. If you're a second language learner, it helps enormously to have the time to process a new idea. This kind of recycling of the same idea many times over, I think is one of the most important things about a curriculum. I called it message abundancy because it seemed to me that there was an abundancy of messages there and many opportunities to understand something.'

In other words, say less but say it more. For example, rather than aiming for four or five lesson outcomes, accept that two covered thoroughly from several angles with time for independent consolidation and review will be of greater value for an EAL student.

Helping students with exam questions

Examinations require students to be able to read with meaning and answer logically in writing, whatever the subject. You therefore need to teach bilingual students who are still developing their English skills two things:

- how to read the questions
- how to write an answer which follows the cues in the questions (in both reading and writing).

These cues are not always made explicit. It is not always the ideas that bilingual learners need, but the language needed for answering the question.

> Students need a wide variety of experiences and texts and a formula on how to write in different genres so that they can confidently apply what they know to any unfamiliar context.

Experience suggests that EAL learners often encounter difficulties with whole-text genre (which usually gains the highest amount of marks) due to a lack of shared cultural assumptions and experiences. Similarly in reading, inference and deduction, text structure, use of language, and writer's purpose and effect on the reader may continue to cause problems well beyond the **new** or **exploring** stages of language learning.

Suggested teaching sequence, sample strategies and activities for EAL development

The teaching sequences suggested within the course materials are supportive of EAL learners' language development as they move through a predictable sequence:

> First, developing familiarity with the context and building on the resources students bring.

> Next, explicitly defining and modelling purpose, function and audience.

> Then, joint construction which highlights and makes explicit language features and grammar associated with the above.

> Finally, independent construction and opportunities for assessment and consolidation.

This approach is consistent with the principles noted on pages 12–13 and is supportive of learners at all stages of acquiring EAL, and is beneficial to *all* learners and not just those learning EAL. This means the teaching sequence is compatible with teaching a class or set which includes bilingual students at various stages of learning English as well as English-only students. The advantage of this approach is that it is flexible enough to accommodate individual learners' needs at varying stages.

The table on pages 17–18 illustrates the teaching sequence, explains why and how this is helpful and highlights some sample strategies. Throughout the Teacher's Guide, activities are provided in various parts of the lessons which exemplify these techniques and help you to make further adaptations to lessons to match your learners' needs.

A glossary of these activities is provided on pages 19–23 which briefly explains how the activity works, why it is useful for bilingual students who are still learning EAL, and the EAL language level of learners (**new**, **exploring** or **consolidating**) who would most benefit.

Lesson phase	Why?	How?	Sample strategies
Introduction Set the context to build field knowledge, including concrete experiences, multimedia input, exploratory talk in L1 and L2, reading and note-making.	• Give students the opportunity to show and build on what they already know about the topic. • Develop students' knowledge and understanding of language and content together. • Ensure students become familiar with the context, structure of the genre and specific and general vocabulary such as names, objects and actions.	• Develop topic/field knowledge and resources by making links with prior knowledge in first language and English. • Consider breaking topics down into more specific sub-topics. • Develop opportunities for 'message abundancy'. • Help learners find ways into the text and use this to generate their own content. • Use and/or provide personal experiences to add to content. • Consider metaphor, idiom and colloquial language which may be problematic.	• Practical experiences • Pre-reading oral activities to set up or predict context • Brainstorming and mind-mapping • Vocabulary chaining • Introducing key visuals, real objects and multimodal introductions • Dictogloss • Focusing on main ideas • Presentations, interactive activities, pairing students with first language English speakers • Using speech bubbles to show the literal meaning of an idiomatic expression in pictorial form to help students see the difference between the word meaning and the intended message
Modelling The teacher models and defines the task, making audience, purpose, form and expected language features explicit.	• Guide the students in exploring the genre and the language features in genre, field, tenor and mode orally. • Language functions/thinking skills such as 'justify', 'compare', 'contrast', 'analyse', 'synthesise' and 'explain', which are required in GCSE English exam tasks, are modelled and scaffolded in context with the appropriate language needed.	• Recognise that register and genre may be different in L1 and use examples to demonstrate this. • Explain and model language functions. • Teach how register varies according to social context and involves the language choices made about what is being discussed (field), the relationship between participants (tenor) and how it is communicated (mode). • Make audience, purpose, form and expected language features explicit.	• Graphic organisers • Key visuals • Concept maps • Functions • Active listening and speaking activities attached to different types of registers • Identifying reference items

Lesson phase	Why?	How?	Sample strategies
Joint construction Move from informal to formal talk, and scaffolding writing. The teacher guides the discussion by asking questions, making suggestions and re-wording or re-casting.	• Students are able to take an increasing role in the joint construction using what they have learnt about the structure and the language features of the genre. • Students develop the oral language skills of pronunciation, intonation, stress and volume.	• Help learners to become meaning seekers and teach strategies to identify, understand and use vocabulary items in source materials, including the movement between general and specific vocabulary. • Explain and scaffold sequencing and structuring conventions. • Provide help with prepositions in formulaic phrases and delexical verbs if needed.	• Identifying key words from sources and using them to generate content • Using connectives • Sequencing activities • Grouping strategies which require students to communicate with their peers • Organising ideas into a logical sequence • Collaborative activities

Independent construction
Students are supported in the task of independent construction by the teacher breaking tasks down into sub-tasks, by grouping strategies and by supporting independent learning.
	• EAL students will need to have several practice attempts and opportunities to peer assess, edit and rewrite before they become competent.
	• Independent construction should be scaffolded by using a range of grouping strategies, frames and aids.
		• Set meaning-making activities.
		• Set activities which develop and scaffold independent meaning-making skills.
		• Tasks may be broken down into smaller tasks such as:
		  – planning a number of paragraphs in a logical sequence
		  – a good introduction for one or several pieces of work in different genres
		  – a good conclusion which links to the introduction.
		• Set tasks which build skills in integrating evidence to justify opinions.
			• Pair and group work
			• Key visuals
			• Graphic organisers
			• Using English and bilingual dictionaries
			• ICT-based tools

Assessment and consolidation Provide ongoing assessment and consolidation of both language and content.	• Making assessment criteria explicit may help students to realise what they have to do to reach higher levels in examinations and progress in their language learning. • Need to assess language and content holistically and separately.	• Provide individual feedback on errors/development points unless these apply to a large number of students. • Sentence-level difficulties for EAL learners may include: subject/verb noun/pronoun agreements and some plurals; articles; endings for tense/person; and modal verbs. • Provide examples of a learning sequence followed by a test and an exemplar answer which shows how the marks awarded increase if certain features are included in the answer. • Take account of examples from recent exam questions and both the KS3 and KS4 marking schemes.	• Assessment strategies which require students to communicate with their peers and provide further opportunities to recycle and consolidate language • Oral and written feedback on both content and language • Visual approaches to identifying how well assessment criteria have been met • Peer and self-assessment strategies

Further resources and reading

Cameron, L. (2003). *Writing in English as an Additional Language at Key Stage 4 and Post-16*. London: Ofsted.

Cummins, J. (1984). *Bilingualism and Special Education: issues in assessment and pedagogy*. Clevedon, England: Multilingual Matters.

Cummins, J. (2001). *Negotiating Identities: Education for Empowerment in a Diverse Society* (2nd edn.). Los Angeles: California Association for Bilingual Education (CABE).

DfEE (2001). *Literacy Across the Curriculum* (DfEE Ref 0235/2001).

Excell, D. (2006). 'Key Stage 3: Observations on Baseline Reading Tests and Formal Assessments for EAL Learners' in *NALDIC Quarterly 4.2*. Reading, England: NALDIC.

Gibbons, P. (2002). *Scaffolding Language, Scaffolding Learning: teaching second language learners in the mainstream classroom*. Portsmouth, New Hampshire, USA: Heinemann.

Gibbons, P. (2008). 'Challenging Pedagogies: More than just good practice' in *NALDIC Quarterly 6.2*. Reading, England: NALDIC.

Halliday, M.A.K. (1975). *Learning How to Mean*. London: Edward Arnold.

Leung, C. (2004). *English as an Additional Language – Language and Literacy Development*. Royston, England: United Kingdom Literacy Association (UKLA).

McWilliam, N. (1998). *What's in a Word?: vocabulary development in multilingual classrooms*. Stoke-on-Trent, England: Trentham.

Mohan, B. (1986). *Language and Content*. Reading, Massachusetts, USA: Addison-Wesley.

Ofsted (2005). *Could they do even better? The writing of advanced bilingual learners of English at Key Stage 2: HMI survey of good practice*. London: Office for Standards in Education.

Royal Borough of Kensington and Chelsea (RBKC). (2006). *English Language and Literacy in Curriculum Learning*. London: RBKC.

Glossary of EAL teaching and learning techniques

Mainly oral

What is the technique?	How to do it?	Why do it?
Visual presentation	The teacher uses an oral, visual and animated presentation to key learners into the topic matter.	EAL learners can quickly learn new vocabulary when they can associate it with a picture or artefact.
Talk partners An organised form of pair work.	Learners are carefully matched in pairs in order to discuss their responses to teacher questions when asked.	EAL beginners can be placed with more able, fluent speakers of English who can model appropriate language use.
Hot seating	Learners are given a character, often with a role-play card to support. A learner who has read and understood his or her character sits in the middle of a circle of learners. Other pupils take it in turns to ask questions of the character who responds in role.	EAL learners hear real language in context. They are able to listen to other fluent speakers. Oral rehearsal develops the exploratory talk of more advanced learners and is good preparation for writing.
L1 discussion	EAL learners are given time to talk about new subject content in their first language with another speaker of the same language.	EAL pupils are able to use subject knowledge learnt in their first language and key into a topic. Sometimes vocabulary is similar, especially in science subjects with Latinate vocabulary.

Oral prediction	Before reading, the teacher asks learners to predict from title, pictures or sub-headings what the text will contain.	This technique requires learners to build on their prior knowledge including how texts work. It helps information retrieval.
Brainstorming or spider diagram	A group of pupils are asked to generate ideas and words related to a (new) topic. These are usually recorded visually by the teacher or another student.	Gives EAL learners a chance to learn key topic vocabulary. Several pupils working together can extend each other's repertoire.
Mind-mapping or concept mapping	This is a systematic type of brainstorm. Pupils link key topic words or concepts into sentences or sentences into paragraphs. The teacher may initially give key words to pupils to find links. These may be colour coded.	Allows EAL learners to build on prior knowledge and transfer learning from their first language.
Collaborative activities	These are any activities in the classroom that require learners to work together and discuss things in order to complete a task (e.g. information gap, envoy, jigsaw).	If the teacher plans groups carefully EAL learners are able to be involved at their own level.
Envoys Pupils carry information from one group to another	A group of three or four learners complete an oral or reading task on topic, for example, describing a character from a book and choosing quotations to illustrate their points. Other groups work on different characters in the same way. After a period of time an envoy from each group is sent to the next group in a clockwise direction and reports to the new group. Then a second envoy goes to the next group and so on until all groups have heard each other's work.	EAL learners hear real language in context. They are able to listen to other fluent speakers.
Washing line A type of evaluative or ranking activity	Pupils are given adjectives or other evaluative statements. They have to arrange the words (or themselves) from strongest to weakest (e.g. fantastic-excellent-good-OK).	This is a good vocabulary expansion activity for more advanced EAL learners. It develops understanding of shades of meaning.
Active listening (e.g. cloze)	Students have a prepared text with words deleted. The teacher reads the complete text and learners listen in order to insert the missing words.	EAL learners get a chance to hear a model text. Depending on which words are omitted they can concentrate on key grammatical or vocabulary items.
Information gap activities or barrier games	There are many types of barrier game. Learners work in pairs. Each learner has a different piece of information (e.g. diagram, picture or text). They both have to complete a single task by asking for, and using information from, the other. So one learner might have a map and draw a route while listening to his or her partner's set of directions.	The barrier or information gap requires real language to be used to complete a task. EAL learners can be paired with supportive, fluent speakers who can help scaffold the task through careful wording or questioning.
Message abundancy The repetition of key words or concepts	The teacher presents the same information in two or more different ways in a lesson, e.g. on a DVD, through text highlighting and while speaking.	EAL learners have several opportunities to pick up and absorb new words, phrases and concepts.

Mainly reading

What is the technique?	How to do it?	Why do it?
Jigsaw reading Groups read different texts and then regroup to feed back	The class is divided into groups of four or five. Each group is given a different text to read and questions or a task about a topic. After the task has been completed, one person from each group comes together to form a new group with information from each text. They can then share their expertise about the topic.	The texts and tasks can be designed for different levels of EAL learner at appropriate reading levels. Emerging EAL learners will be supported by working collaboratively.
Underlining/ highlighting Learners use highlighters to mark different aspects of a text	Learners are given a complete text with instructions to highlight key aspects. These can be: grammatical, such as underlining past tense verbs in blue and time connectives (conjunctions) in red; semantic, e.g. all the nouns relating to time; or content-based (e.g. all the sentences describing a character).	The technique draws learners' attention to the form and structure of texts at sentence or paragraph level.
Identifying reference items	The teacher highlights reference words in a non-fiction text (e.g. pronouns: it, this, these, theirs). Learners have to identify and highlight the nouns to which they refer.	This helps more advanced EAL learners focus on the difficult process of cohesion and back referencing. It draws attention to how texts work.
Matching activities Learners have to match words and definitions or two parts of a sentence	Words and definitions are printed on card which is then cut up. Learners work in pairs to match them up.	Through working together learners can practise using new vocabulary. Being able to move and manipulate text helps identify key language patterns.
Sequencing Learners have to reassemble or sequence a cut-up text	A complete text printed on card is cut up. Learners work in pairs to reassemble the original text in the correct sequence.	Learners understand how a text works and begin to use their knowledge of key grammatical items such as conjunctions and pronouns which link sentences and paragraphs.
Relevance sorting Learners have a set of cards with key points about a particular question, e.g. What were the causes of the First World War?	The key question is written in the centre of concentric circles. Pupils place their supporting evidence cards around the centre with the most relevant points nearer to the centre.	This is a useful planning strategy for essay writing in English or Humanities subjects. It enables learners to prioritise and organise the writing of longer texts.
Ranking and justifying activities (e.g. Diamond Nine)	Learners are given a set of cards to evaluate in some way. For example, deciding which character is most to blame for an event in a narrative. They must arrange the cards in order from best to worst. In a Diamond Nine there are always nine cards which must be ordered into a diamond pattern.	EAL learners hear the language of justification and evaluation. It supports EAL learners in bridging talk and writing.

Joint construction Various activities that involve the teacher guiding learners in how texts work	The teacher or other students model how to read a text, such as skimming and scanning, or how to write a paragraph with a topic sentence and supporting evidence.	Helps EAL learners to become meaning seekers and teaches strategies to identify, understand and use vocabulary items in source materials. They can take an increasing role in the joint construction using what they have learnt about the language features of a new genre.

Mainly writing

What is the technique?	How to do it?	Why do it?
Cloze A specialised form of gap filling	A text is prepared with one type of word omitted, e.g. all nouns, all verbs. It can also be used for learning new subject vocabulary.	Supports EAL learners in looking at semantic patterns or sentence structures such as past tenses, prepositions.
Selective cloze	A text is prepared with every seventh or eighth word deleted (or every tenth if it is for beginners). Learners collaborate in pairs to find suitable replacements for the omitted words.	Helpful for teachers to assess learners' comprehension of more complex texts. If they cannot get about 80% correct the text is too difficult.
Dictogloss A supported dictation	This is a listening and writing activity. The teacher chooses a short text on a topic that is familiar to the learners (about 100 words for EAL beginners and intermediates). The teacher reads the text aloud while learners listen. On the second and third readings learners may write notes. Next, pupils work in pairs and then fours to try to reconstruct the original text.	Learners hear a model text on a familiar topic. They collaborate to reconstruct complex sentences and scaffold each other's learning.
Sentence starters	The teacher prepares a topic-specific list of key sentence patterns for learners to use. An extended version of this technique, covering a complete text, would be a writing frame (see below).	This is best for beginner and developing EAL learners who are unsure of how to start writing.
Writing frames	The writing frame is best used as a genre-specific scaffold. The teacher usually provides key connectives and linking phrases.	Emerging EAL learners are supported to link together short simple sentences into complex sentences and paragraphs.
Key visuals or graphic organisers	Key visuals are a type of graphic organiser. They are used to show the underlying structure of a text: e.g. a flow chart signifies a sequential text, a two-way table can illustrate an argument for and against, or a tree diagram can classify scientific information. Teachers can either use the visual to help students make notes while reading about a topic or use the visual and notes as a plan and preparation for writing.	The use of visual organisers helps EAL learners see the underlying structure, form and purpose of key genres of English writing.

What is the technique?	How to do it?	Why do it?
ICT-based tools (e.g. bilingual dictionaries and thesauruses)	Apart from the use of book-based thesauruses and dictionaries, Microsoft Word can be used to great effect. Learners highlight and then right-click on a word and select 'synonyms' or definitions. A dialogue box will appear with other suggested words with a similar meaning.	Emerging and consolidating EAL pupils need to expand their vocabulary as fast as possible. Using a bilingual dictionary supports the transfer of learning from first language into English.
Substitution tables	The teacher provides model sentences with various choices in a tabular form. Learners generate their own sentence following the set patterns. 	Today Yesterday Tomorrow	is / will be / was	sunny. cloudy. snowing. thundery.
---	---	---		The technique enables EAL pupils to focus on form and write accurate grammatical sentences while also having some vocabulary and content choice.
Peer-assessment strategies	When a first draft of a text has been written, learners swap their writing and read and comment on its effectiveness or mark work according to agreed success criteria.	It provides further opportunities to recycle and consolidate language and encourages real life communication with peers.
Oral and written feedback on both content and language	Teachers mark work with specific grammatical or linguistic foci, e.g. in a narrative text, requiring learners to have consistent use of the past tense, or in an argumentative text, to use a range of modal verbs.	The technique draws attention to the form and structure of texts. It can help EAL learners to realise what they have to do to reach higher levels in examinations and progress in their language learning.
Visual approaches to identify how well assessment criteria have been met	During class work, especially during the listening phase at the start of a lesson, the teacher asks learners to display coloured cards to show whether they have understood. Green signifies the student is confident, amber means not sure and red means no understanding. (Also known as traffic light system.)	EAL learners may be initially reluctant to ask for help. This gives them a less threatening way of signalling a lack of comprehension.
Self-assessment checklists	Students mark a self-assessment check sheet with ✓, ✗ or O to show whether they have understood.	EAL learners may be initially reluctant to ask for help. This gives them a less threatening way of signalling comprehension or lack of it.

'List or find' questions
Teaching and learning and GradeStudio

Learning Objectives
- to select relevant details from a passage
- to present details clearly using a list or prose

Required resources
- Student Book, pages 10–13
- Worksheet 1.1: 'List or find' questions
- Worksheet 1.2: 'List' sample responses
- Worksheet 1.3: Examiner's comments on the sample responses

Assessment Objectives
Read and understand texts, selecting material appropriate to purpose, collating from different sources and making comparisons and cross-references as appropriate (English AO2i; English Language AO3i)

1 Starter

Distribute copies of **Worksheet 1.1**, which contains introductory tasks on 'List or find' questions. Students complete tasks 1 and 2 in pairs, discussing their ideas and feeding back to the class after each part has been completed.

Students complete task 3 independently. Take feedback to consolidate and ensure understanding.

Worksheet 1.1

Worksheet 1.1

2 Whole-class work

Use page 10 of the Student Book to reinforce the learning from the Starter activity.

Using the sample answer on **Worksheet 1.1**, model how to turn a 'List' answer into continuous prose: emphasise the need for full sentences – all ideas should be introduced properly, and linking words and phrases such as 'also' and 'further on in the article' need to be used to connect the different pieces of evidence fluently.

Turn to the Bill Bryson extract on page 11 of the Student Book and introduce Activity 1 on page 10.

Begin the reading and encourage students to identify evidence in the text in answer to the question. Using students' suggestions, highlight this evidence using the annotation tool on the ActiveTeach CD-ROM.

Once three or four pieces of evidence have been identified, invite suggestions to begin a 'List' and a continuous prose answer for display (either written on a whiteboard or typed on a computer and projected).

Recap key points about this kind of question and answer.

3 Independent work

Students finish reading the extract, then produce answers for tasks 1 and 2 of Activity 1.

4 Peer/Self-assessment

Distribute copies of **Worksheet 1.2**, which contains two sample 'List' responses.

Students consider which response is stronger, and how they know this, then annotate the answers with their ideas.

Students feed back their conclusions.

Distribute **Worksheet 1.3**, which contains the accompanying Examiner comments. Students check their conclusions against the examiner comments.

With the class, establish key steps to use when assessing 'List' questions (e.g. count the number of points provided; check that each point is a new idea).

Students swap responses to Activity 1, task 1 and peer-assess each other's work using the key steps. Ask: Would the marking steps be different for 'Find' questions that require you to write in continuous prose?

Turn to page 13 of the Student Book. Students read the C-grade answer and the accompanying examiner comments. Ask students to reflect: what makes a successful continuous prose answer to a 'list or find' question?

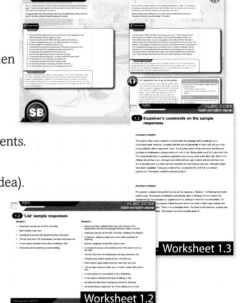

Worksheet 1.3

Worksheet 1.2

5 Interactive GradeStudio

Open the interactive GradeStudio activity using ActiveTeach.

The objective of this activity is for students to understand the mark scheme.

Use this activity at the front of the class to assess sample answers at every grade, using the highlight tool and questions to assess the strengths and weaknesses of the answers. Students put themselves in the position of the examiner and reward the sample answers with a grade.

6 Further work

For homework, students find an article similar to 'Help! It's the scare bear bunch' and devise a 'List' or 'Find' question to go with it. The article and question will be given to a peer to read and answer.

Suggested answers

Activity 1, task 1, page 10

1. Every twenty minutes on the Appalachian Trail, Bryson and Katz walked further than the average American walks in a week.

2. Americans use the car for 93% of all trips, whatever the distance or purpose.

3. In Hanover, walking is easy but almost no-one walks anywhere for anything.

4. Bryson's neighbour drives 800 yards to work.

5. A perfectly 'fit' woman will drive 100 yards to pick up her child.

6. Virtually every child gets picked up from school by car.

7. Most children aged sixteen years or older have their own cars.

8. On average the total walking of an American is 1.4 miles a week (or 350 yards a day).

9. In many places in America, it is not possible to be a pedestrian.

10. The man in Waynesboro seems shocked at the idea of Bryson walking a mile.

11. He takes the joke about emergency provisions seriously.

12. He wishes Bryson 'good luck'.

'List or find' questions
Exam practice and assessment

Learning Objectives
- to practise selecting relevant details
- to develop a secure approach to 'List or find' questions

Required resources
- Student Book, pages 14–15
- Worksheet 1.4: Criticisms of zoos

Assessment Objectives
Read and understand texts, selecting material appropriate to purpose, collating from different sources and making comparisons and cross-references as appropriate (English AO2i; English Language AO3i)

1 Starter
Using page 14 of the Student Book, introduce Activity 1 and read the extract 'Sad Eyes and Empty Lives'.

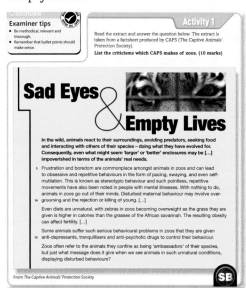

Distribute copies of **Worksheet 1.4**, which contains a sample 'list' response for students to assess and improve. Explain the task using the instructions on the worksheet. Students complete the task in pairs. After 5 minutes, take feedback, encouraging students to refer to their learning from the previous lesson to support their comments.

Worksheet 1.4

2 Whole-class/paired work
Remind the class that as Higher Tier students, they are more likely to be presented with a 'Find' than a 'List' question.

Ask students to re-word the question in Activity 1 so that it asks for a continuous prose response. Take feedback and agree on a new question. In pairs, students produce a continuous prose answer to this new question.

Pairs swap responses with another pair and peer-assess their answer, highlighting effective words and phrases used to create the continuous prose response.

Take feedback and write responses on the board, creating a bank of words and phrases for students to use to create fluent and coherent continuous prose responses.

Starter
- **Activate prior knowledge** by recapping ideas covered in the previous lesson. Extend if possible. Use **message abundancy** to clarify 'relevant, methodical… thorough' in the Examiner tips and 'criticisms' in the question.

Activity 1
- **Talk partners**: pair EAL students with good L1 English students to read through the text and discuss challenging vocabulary such as: 'predators', 'enclosures', 'impoverished', 'obsessive', 'self-mutilation', 'tranquillisers'…to aid understanding as

appropriate. Dictionaries could be useful. Ask students to highlight words and phrases which suggest criticism as preparation for a 'methodical' answer.
- **Collaborative activities**: groups/pairs use **joint construction** of continuous prose. Suggestions for sentence starters could be useful.

Activity 2
- **Oral prediction**: invent a title for the Carmen Glatt text which would enable students to predict the content. It could be beneficial for EAL students for the teacher or strong English speakers to read the passage to the class (or EAL student(s), to clarify words/phrases such as 'conscientiously', 'no slouch', 'no match'…as appropriate, to aid understanding).

3 Independent work
Students write their answers to Activity 2 on page 15 of the Student Book.

Activity 2

Read the extract and answer the question below.

According to this article, what actions has Carmen Glatt taken to show her concern about pollution and the environment?
(10 marks)

The day of the Eco-Pests
By Paul Vallely

Adults are unwise to try drinking water from the tap while Carmen Glatt is around. Carmen is only eleven but nobody could question her clarity of vision or her determination. She is very aware that all the water we drink is recycled, says her mum, and she is convinced that anything which comes out of a tap must be polluted in some way. She conscientiously changes the family's water filter every week.

'If someone gets a drink of water from the tap she says "No, No, No" and throws it away and gets some from the filter. She washes all salad and fruit with filtered water,' says her mother. As a nutritionist, Mrs Glatt is no slouch on health matters but she admits she is no match for her daughter [...]

And it is not just the water. There is air pollution too. 'She even bought a breathing filter for her father for when he cycles to the office,' says Mrs Glatt, clearly both simultaneously overwhelmed and impressed by her daughter's tenacity. 'And he has to buy unleaded petrol,' she adds.

When it comes to shopping Carmen accompanies her mother to the supermarket to supervise the family purchases. 'She reads the packages of everything and watches out for certain chemicals or artificial sweeteners. She won't have certain kinds of apples because she says they taste of chemical...

4 Plenary
Partners swap responses to Activity 2 and mark each other's work, using the instructions on page 15 of the Student Book. Students feed back comments to each other.

Students self-assess their personal strengths, and identify a target area to improve.

Peer/Self-assessment

1 Check your answers to Activities 1 and 2.
- Did you find enough clear points?
- Did you present and organise your answer in the appropriate way?

2 Now try to grade your answer to Activities 1 and 2 by applying what you learnt in GradeStudio. You will need to be careful and precise in your marking.

Tick each clearly made, supported point. For a question like this, the total number of ticks will produce, or strongly influence, the final mark.

↑ Moving up the grades

A*	9/10 ticks
A	8 ticks
B	7 ticks
C	5/6 ticks
D	4 ticks

Suggested answers

Activity 1, page 14
- Even larger enclosures do not meet animals' real needs.
- Frustration and boredom are commonplace for zoo animals.
- This boredom can lead to 'obsessive and repetitive behaviours', similar to those observed in people with mental illnesses.
- The animals pace up and down.
- The animals sway from side-to-side.
- The animals self-mutilate.
- The animals go out of their minds because they have nothing to do.
- Maternal behaviour is disturbed.
- Mothers 'over-groom'.
- Mothers may reject or kill their young.
- Zoo animals' diets are unnatural.
- Zebras become overweight because they are fed grass, which is relatively high in calories.
- Obesity can affect fertility.
- Some zoo animals are given drugs to control their behaviour.
- The conditions are unnatural.

Activity 2, page 15
- She 'changes the family's water filter every week'.
- She refuses tap water.
- She won't let anyone else drink it.
- 'She washes all salad and fruit with filtered water.'
- She bought a 'breathing filter for her father'
- She insists on unleaded petrol.
- She supervises the family shopping.
- She reads the packages of everything.
- She watches out for certain chemicals or artificial sweeteners.
- She won't have certain kinds of apples because they taste of chemicals.

'Evidence' questions
Teaching and learning

Learning Objectives

- to select relevant evidence from a passage
- to organise the evidence into a coherent response

Required resources

- Student Book, pages 16–17
- Video clip 1.1: *Dragons' Den* footage
- Worksheet 1.5: 'Evidence' questions
- Worksheet 1.6: 'Evidence' questions – suggested answers

Assessment Objectives

Read and understand texts, selecting material appropriate to purpose, collating from different sources and making comparisons and cross-references as appropriate (English AO2i; English Language AO3i)

1 Starter

Recap: What key ingredients of 'Locate and retrieve' questions have we established so far?

Introduce **Video clip 1.1** by asking: What evidence does the presenter use to suggest to the Dragons that his product deserves investment?

Watch the clip. Students independently note the evidence they spot.

Video 1.1

Take feedback, writing students' responses on the board.

Watch the clip again to ensure all evidence was spotted and then listed in the same order as on the video.

2 Whole-class/paired work

Introduce page 16 of the Student Book and explain the Learning Objectives.

My learning objectives ▼
- to select relevant evidence from a passage
- to organise the evidence into a coherent response.
SB

Read the instructions for Activity 1 and the Orwell extract.

Distribute copies of **Worksheet 1.5**, which contains a sample answer for Activity 1 with blank spaces for students to complete evidence from the Orwell extract. Students complete task 1 on the worksheet in pairs.

After 10–15 minutes, pairs swap responses with another pair to peer-assess. Students should check that the evidence used is appropriate and makes sense.

Give students 2–3 minutes to complete task 2 on the worksheet independently.

Take feedback to consolidate and ensure understanding.

Suggested answers are provided on **Worksheet 1.6**.

Starter
- The advice given in the teachers' notes and the introduction of the student book will all be helpful for EAL students. Use **message abundancy** to clarify appropriate words throughout the lesson, e.g. 'editing', 'investment', 'integrating'... .
- **Talk partners**: establish the idea of 'evidence' by activating previous knowledge of the word in other contexts – remind students of the PEE technique, where one E stands for Evidence (or quotations).
- Some EAL students may have no prior knowledge of *Dragon's Den* so **hot seating** could be used to aid understanding of the cultural background.

Activity 1
- **Active Listening**: the teacher or fluent English speakers should read the text with pauses, expression, gestures and facial expression to aid understanding.
- The exemplar **underlining/highlighting** shows very clearly that 'evidence' should be short and relevant. Worksheet 1.5 provides the very useful **writing frame** to model 'integrating' the evidence. **Joint construction** of one or two sentences would also be helpful as a scaffold towards more independent work in Activity 1 (and ultimately in exams).

3 Independent work
Students complete Activity 2 on page 17 of the Student Book.

Suggested answers
Suggested answers to **Worksheet 1.5** are provided on **Worksheet 1.6**.

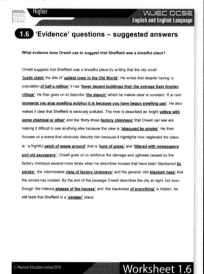

Activity 2, task 1, page 17
- He suggests that the problem is nationwide from Cornwall to Cumbria.
- The waste is 'a mountain', suggesting its large scale.
- He claims that rubbish is everywhere – it is 'wherever you look'.
- He then lists the items that litter the 'beautiful' countryside such as 'rusting fridges, plastic bags and old prams'.
- He uses the word 'plague' to suggest that litter is spreading like an infectious disease. He uses personal experience (calling the council every week).
- He uses the shocking statistic of £400 million just to clean up the litter.
- He describes Britain as 'consumerist and throwaway', a place where it is 'normal' to get rid of items before they are really useless.
- 90 million 'dumped' phones is a staggering statistic.
- He draws attention to all the packaging on consumer items – it is likely to be 'chucked', not recycled.
- 100 million tons of rubbish thrown away each year by homes and businesses is another dramatic statistic.
- The reference to filling Trafalgar Square to the top of Nelson's Column is a dramatic illustration of the scale of the problem.
- He ends by insisting that there is increasing dumping on verges, streets and fields.

4 Plenary
Ask students to consider the 'key ingredients' list from the beginning of the lesson and decide whether anything new can now be added. Add any appropriate suggestions.

'Evidence' questions
GradeStudio and Assessment

Required resources
• Student Book, pages 18–21

Learning Objectives
• to practise selecting relevant evidence
• to develop a secure approach to this type of question

Assessment Objectives
Read and understand texts, selecting material appropriate to purpose, collating from different sources and making comparisons and cross-references as appropriate (English AO2i; English Language AO3i)

1 Starter

Using ActiveTeach, display Student 2 and Student 3's responses to the question for Activity 2. Students work in pairs to decide which response is stronger and why.

Take feedback, encouraging focused explanations of why one answer is stronger than the other.

2 Whole-class work

Using GradeStudio on pages 18–19 of the Student Book, students compare the responses they wrote in the last lesson for Activity 2 with the sample responses provided. They should read the examiner comments carefully.

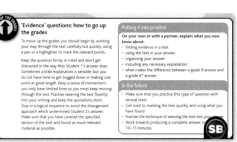

Students decide which grade they are working at and what they need to do to improve. Take feedback to share and compare progress.

Ask: What is rewarded in this sort of question? Emphasise the examiner's key points and write them on the whiteboard as a checklist:
• consistent focus on the question
• methodical tracking of the text
• explanation where necessary
• enough relevant material used
• fluency and coherence.

Students choose and write out one area from the checklist as a target to focus on to improve their responses.

3 Interactive GradeStudio

Open the interactive GradeStudio activity using ActiveTeach.

The objective of this activity is to understand what skills are required at different grades, and that there are different ways to achieve the same grade. This activity gives a range of sample answers for each grade.

At the front of the class analyse and compare the answers to the same grade, and compare the answer at different grades.

Discuss the examiner comments with the class so that students can understand what skills are required at each grade and see that there are different ways to achieve the same grade.

Students will become familiar with the criteria specific to each grade. Students will also be shown the best way to arrive at that grade. In addition, by comparing answers to the same question the students can see how questions are commonly misinterpreted and marks are lost.

⦿ EAL additional support

Starter
- The ticks are a very clear visual method of showing the development of answers from Grade E to A*. Clarify any words in the Examiner summaries or 'putting it into practice' sections as appropriate.
- **Talk partners**: ask a fluent English speaker to annotate an EAL student's response using the examiner's words.
- The same pairs could also make a mind map of each of the three student answers in the Student Book, pages 18–19 as a way of showing why 3 is better than 2 is better than 1. This would also be useful when analysing and assessing their own answers.
- The A* answer could be made into a **dictogloss** activity as an exemplar of the standard of writing required.

Activity 1
- **Visual presentation**: use an encyclopaedia or similar text with pictures of different types of fish to **activate prior knowledge** before reading the exam practice text on pages 20–21.
- Read the question and as a class discuss the key words to ensure understanding.

4 Independent work

Students complete the practice question in Activity 1 independently.

After 15 minutes, they self-check their answers as advised in the Student Book.

5 Peer/Self-assessment

Partners swap responses and peer-assess each other's work using the class checklist (see Box 2, Whole-class work) .

Students feed back their comments to each other.

Students evaluate how successfully they addressed their own targets.

6 Further work

For homework, students create a poster explaining their ideas in response to the 'what you know about' bullet points (in the 'Putting it into practice' box) on page 19 of the Student Book.

Suggested answers

Activity 1, page 20
- fish and animals suffer sickness, distress and physical abuse
- animals are kept which are scarred and deformed
- they behave abnormally
- they are routinely mishandled by staff and visitors
- a starfish lost a limb through mishandling
- children throw diseased crabs into pools
- sharks are held out of the water so they can be touched
- staff force rays to swim out of the water to feed
- staff train rays and sharks to behave abnormally
- few aquariums are involved in genuine marine conservation
- 80% of aquarium animals are caught in the wild
- very few are used in breeding programmes
- tens of thousands of fish die in aquariums
- thousands die in transit
- fish are frequently ill or malnourished
- they use conservation as a 'convenient veneer'
- they regard animals as 'disposable'

'Explain' questions
Teaching and learning and GradeStudio

Learning Objectives
- to learn how to approach 'Explain' questions
- to practise explaining a writer's ideas and perspectives

Required resources
- Student Book, pages 22–25
- Photo 1.1: Two men being admired
- Worksheet 1.7: Evidence and inference
- Worksheet 1.8: Grade B sample response
- Worksheet 1.9: 'Explain' questions – bad answers

Assessment Objectives
Read and understand texts, selecting material appropriate to purpose, collating from different sources and making comparisons and cross-references as appropriate (English AO2i; English Language AO3i)

1 Starter
Using ActiveTeach, display photograph 1.1 and distribute copies to the class.

Ask: What do the women think of this man? How can we tell? Students discuss in pairs. After 2 minutes, take feedback. Using the whiteboard, annotate the photograph with students' ideas (*e.g. circle the smile on a woman's face – she obviously likes what she sees.*)

Explain that we have just used inference and deduction to 'read' the picture and understand the messages within it. This involves searching the text for clues and then putting those clues together and 'reading between the lines' to gain an understanding of any underlying meanings in the text.

Highlight which parts of the annotation were textual clues and which were inferences (*e.g. the smile is a clue; 'she likes him' an inference*). Emphasise that textual clues need to be precise, and that inferences involve using your own, effective vocabulary and phrasing to show your understanding of those clues.

Ask: How could you transfer the skills you used to read the photograph, to reading a text? Take suggestions, writing any useful ideas on the board.

2 Whole-class work

Introduce page 22 of the Student Book and explain the Learning Objectives. Read the exam question and the extract about Fogle and Cracknell.

Ask students to look at Activity 1, task 1 on page 23 of the Student Book.

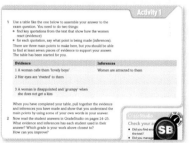

Distribute copies of **Worksheet 1.7**, which contains the evidence and inference table from Activity 1 on page 23 of the Student Book. Students identify where in the table they can see an example of each of the two things they have been advised to do in Activity 1, task 1.

With the class, model the further selection of evidence and the interpretation in the inference column.

EAL additional support

Starter

- The photograph is a **visual presentation** which is very supportive for EAL students. Pictures of optical illusions are useful for helping students to see more than one way of looking at something.
- **Talk partners**: pair an EAL student with a fluent English speaker to establish/confirm the understanding of key words such as 'inference', 'clarity coherence'.
- **Sequencing**: establish the idea of following an argument.

Activity 1

- EAL students should work through the Fogle/Cracknell text, picking out words they're not sure about and use a dictionary and thesaurus to find definitions and common collocations to avoid literal interpretations of idiomatic language, e.g. 'tweed suit', 'eyes riveted', 'swoon'…
- Other useful approaches could be a spider diagram for attaching evidence to questions and **relevance sorting**. Students could work in groups to construct a simple set of cards, one card to describe a situation, the others being explanations of the situation. Groups exchange sets to sort.

3 Independent work

Students work independently to complete **Worksheet 1.7**. After 10 minutes and still working independently, students move on to Activity 1, task 2, where they use GradeStudio (on pages 24–25 of the Student Book) to assess how well they managed the 'Evidence and inference' exercise.

Worksheet 1.8 includes a further B-grade answer and examiner comments to support the GradeStudio content on pages 24–25 of the Student Book.

2 Now read the student answers in GradeStudio on pages 24–25. What evidence and inferences has each student used in their answer? Which grade is your work above closest to? How can you improve?

Worksheet 1.8

4 Plenary

Using ActiveTeach, display **Worksheet 1.9** and distribute copies to the class. The worksheet contains weak sample answers.

Based on their learning today, students identify the weaknesses in each answer, and suggest improvements.

Using the whiteboard, annotate the answers with students' ideas, using these to reinforce the key learning points from today's lesson. Students follow the annotations on their worksheets.

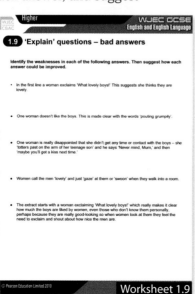

Worksheet 1.9

Suggested answers

Activity 1, task 1, page 23

Evidence	Inferences
1 A woman calls them 'lovely boys'	1 Women are attracted to them
2 Her eyes are 'riveted' to them	
3 A woman is 'grumpy' and disappointed when she does not get a kiss	
4 Female staff are 'excited' and 'assemble, just to gaze'	2 They are the centre of attention – women can't keep their eyes off the men
5 The men cause a 'commotion' amongst the women	
6 'ladies swoon' in their presence	
7 400 women simultaneously started rooting in their bags for lipstick	3 Women want to impress them

'Explain' questions
Exam practice and assessment

Required resources
- Student Book, pages 26–29
- Worksheet 1.10: Reasons for entering the race
- Worksheet 1.11: Reasons for entering the race – answers

Learning Objectives
- to practise 'Explain' questions
- to learn how to combine evidence and inference

Assessment Objectives
Read and understand texts, selecting material appropriate to purpose, collating from different sources and making comparisons and cross-references as appropriate (English AO2i; English Language AO3i)

1 Starter
Use pages 26–27 of the Student Book to introduce Activity 1, then distribute copies of **Worksheet 1.10**, which contains the table from the activity. Give students 10 minutes to complete the table in pairs.

2 Whole-class/paired work
Using ActiveTeach, display the completed grid on **Worksheet 1.11**. Pairs swap their completed worksheets with another pair and peer-assess the responses against the answers in the displayed grid.

Model how to turn the ideas in the grid into continuous prose: remind students to use wording from the question to start their answer, to use linking words and phrases such as 'also' and 'further on in the text' to connect their ideas clearly, and to use words such as 'which suggests' after quotations to effectively explain what the evidence shows us.

Reinforce the key features of this kind of answer, and the skills required to produce a response:

- methodical tracking of the text
- careful selection of the most relevant evidence
- appropriate use of own words to develop and show understanding of the main points.

Worksheet 1.10

1.10 Reasons for entering the race

Explain why Fogle and Cracknell took part in this race. (10 marks)

Fogle		Cracknell	
Evidence	Inference	Evidence	Inference

Worksheet 1.11

1.11 Reasons for entering the race – answers

Explain why Fogle and Cracknell took part in this race. (10 marks)

Fogle		Cracknell	
Evidence	Inference	Evidence	Inference
For the 'huge buzz'	It's exciting	He is a 'two-time Olympic gold medallist at rowing'	He's an expert
Not wanting to only be seen as the 'presenter of Cash in the Attic'	Wanting a different image/wanting to show a different side of himself	There is 'confusion over his future career'	He's not sure what to do next in his career
He says there's 'more to me outside of that little sphere'	Wanting to show what he is capable of	He has found 'Stopping sport ... an incredibly tough thing'	Finding it difficult to give up sport
		Not having to 'grow up'	It's fun
		To 'use the time away' to 'think things through'	Wanting some time and space to help him make the right decisions

Starter/Activity 1
- The table is a helpful way of visualising for comparison – ensure that the pairings are **talk partners** (EAL students paired with fluent English speakers). Clarify cultural or idiomatic words by **message abundancy** as the passage is read out.
- The lesson is EAL friendly by modelling the changing of text from one form to another. It is useful to build a word wall of useful phrases for writing 'explain' responses – many more than are mentioned in

stage d) of whole-class work. If the words are removable, students (or the teacher) can select relevant ones for answering future questions as well as the ones in this lesson.

Activity 2
- To aid independent work use **active listening** where the teacher or several fluent readers read the passage on waste, jotting down unknown words, e.g. 'glitzier', 'woo', 'fly-tipping', 'spate', 'ditches', 'on the up' to discuss as a class later.
- **Highlight** key words in the question to ensure EAL students in particular understand the task.

3 Independent work

Turn to pages 28–29 of the Student Book and introduce Activity 2. Students spend 10 minutes creating and completing their own grid to gather ideas, then write their answer to the question.

4 Plenary

Using page 29 of the Student Book, students self-assess their answer against the bullet points. They then swap answers with a partner and peer-assess them using the mark scheme.

Ask: What must you remember to do in order to complete 'Explain' questions successfully?

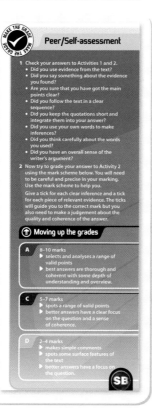

5 Further work

For homework, students create their own 'examiner tips' to help future students complete 'explain' questions successfully.

Suggested answers

Activity 2, pages 28–29

Evidence	Inferences
'Retailers are locked in a bitter struggle to woo customers – glitzier packaging'	Packaging is not going to be reduced and will be made of materials that are harder to recycle
'European Union regulations will trigger more fly-tipping'	Because it will be more difficult, and a more involved process, to get rid of old electronic goods 'legally', people will dump these things illegally
'EU law will require the toxins [electronic goods] contain to be removed and the rest recycled'	
'EU law treats old cars as toxic waste and demands they be disposed of by a specialist'	Getting rid of waste will become expensive
'You have to pay' to have your 'old banger' taken away	People would be unwilling/unable to pay and would find other ways of dumping old cars
Problems in enforcing EU laws	People will just ignore the regulations, and the EU doesn't have the policing structure necessary to enforce these laws
Britain has a poor record for recycling – 'we continue to bury our rubbish out of sight and out of mind'	We already have a poor record for recycling, and a 'head in the sand' approach to waste. Without a change of attitude, the problem can only get worse

'What impressions?' questions
Teaching and learning and GradeStudio

Learning Objectives
- to understand how texts attempt to present an impression of their subject
- to learn how to approach this type of question

Required resources
- Student Book, pages 30–33
- Video clip 1.2: Breakfast news
- Worksheet 1.12: Impressions
- Worksheet 1.13: What impressions…?
- Worksheet 1.14: What impressions…? Sample answer

Assessment Objectives
Read and understand texts, selecting material appropriate to purpose, collating from different sources and making comparisons and cross-references as appropriate (English AO2i; English Language AO3i)

1 Starter

Distribute **Worksheet 1.12** and introduce **Video clip 1.2** with the question: what impression of teenagers do you think the item creates? Watch the video clip and discuss students' responses as a whole class.

Watch the video clip again so that students can focus on *how* this impression is created, noting their thoughts on **Worksheet 1.12**.

After watching the clips, take feedback, compiling students' ideas on the board and encouraging them to make links between each impression and how it was created. Look for responses which recognise that: the presenters give a negative impression of teenagers with their introductory questions; a range of vox pops suggest balance, but the image framing these (*Me Generation*) does not; that the guest 'experts' on the studio do not support the initial impression given by the presenters.

Explain that students will now be considering how writing choices can also create particular impressions.

Worksheet 1.12

Video 1.2

2 Whole-class/paired work

Using ActiveTeach, display the headline 'The sunshine isle where teenage tearaways are sent to learn a lesson'. Ask: What impression is being created of teenagers in this headline? How is that impression being created? Take suggestions.

THE SUNSHINE ISLE WHERE TEENAGE TEARAWAYS ARE SENT TO LEARN A LESSON

Explain that students are now going to hear the rest of the article. Read the article to the students. As they listen, they should list the different impressions that are created of the teenagers. They can use the suggestions already made, based on the headline, to start their list.

After reading, allow pairs/groups 2–3 minutes to share ideas to help develop their lists.

Turn to pages 30–31 of the Student Book and ask students to find a specific word or phrase that helped to create one of the impressions they have written down.

Take feedback, encouraging students to explain how the words and phrases in the article created the impression they have identified.

Starter
- **L1 discussion**: EAL students who share the same L1 could explore the literal, physical meaning of the word 'impression' – such as a coin pressed into clay – as a lead into things that leave an impression in your mind.

Introduction/Whole-class work

Activity 1
- **Visual presentation**: use the photo on page 31 of the Student Book to elicit impressions given by this kind of landscape. To aid understanding, ask the students to consider their five senses.

- **Oral prediction**: before reading the text on pages 30-31, present the photo of the beach and a picture of young people behaving badly. Ask the students to predict how they might be linked.
- **Active listening**: teacher or fluent student readers should take turns to read part of the story using expression, pauses, facial expression and perhaps gestures to aid understanding. Clarify any difficult socio-cultural words with **message abundancy** such as 'tearaway', 'notorious', 'reggae', 'dormitories'…
- The lesson supports EAL learners through clear steps leading to an exam answer and assessment.

3 Independent work

Introduce Activity 1 on pages 30–31 of the Student Book. Distribute copies of **Worksheet 1.13**, which contains a grid for students to record the words or phrases that are linked to their impressions. Students complete the grid. Once completed, students can complete the exam question in task 3 of Activity 1.

Worksheet 1.13

4 Plenary

Display/distribute **Worksheet 1.14**, which shows the sample answer to the question about the teenagers on the Divert Trust scheme. Give students 2–3 minutes to write comments about the sample answer as if they were the examiner. Then get them to stick these comments around the projected answer on the whiteboard, explaining why they have made their choice.

Worksheet 1.14

Once all students have placed their comments, make any necessary changes. Then ask students to use their knowledge of good exam answers to consider what grade this answer would get, and why they think this.

Using ActiveTeach, display Student 2's sample answer (the A* grade), located on page 33 of the Student Book. Ask students to consider what this answer and these comments show about what is needed in these answers. Take feedback to consolidate and ensure understanding.

5 Further work

For homework ask students to find an article about a person or place where a particular impression is created. Students should think up their own exam-style 'What impressions?' question to go with this article, which they then can give to a peer to try out. Students should also think up the mark scheme, so that they will be able to assess their peer's work.

Suggested answers

Activity 1, task 2, page 30

What impressions do we get of the teenagers?	What details from the passage give us this impression?
They are troublemakers/ unruly	'notorious teenage tearaways' (note that some candidates will be prepared to look at 'notorious' and 'tearaways' separately)
Their behaviour is extreme/the worst have bad reputations/rebels	'the most disruptive'
No respect for authority/ rude/horrid	Catalogue of crime (truancy, disrupting lessons, disobeying teachers, breaking school rules)
Lazy	No interest in school work and school activities
Out of control	School governor says nobody can deal with them
Ungrateful/ inconsiderate/self-centred	Sister Celia Cools-Lartigue says they are noisy and they are fussy eaters
They cannot be trusted	They are being closely supervised
There are others who are even worse	They were the best (7 out of 19)
They are being rewarded for their poor behaviour	Governors are annoyed about the scheme 'almost rewarding badly-behaved children'

'What impressions?' questions
Exam practice and assessment

Learning Objectives
- to practise 'What impressions?' questions
- to develop a secure technique for answering these questions

Required resources
- Student Book, pages 34–37
- Worksheet 1.15: What impression of the Duchess…?
- Worksheet 1.16: What impression of the Duchess…? – suggested answers
- Worksheet 1.17: Cracknell's impressions of the race – suggested answers

Assessment Objectives
Read and understand texts, selecting material appropriate to purpose, collating from different sources and making comparisons and cross-references as appropriate (English AO2i; English Language AO3i)

1 Starter
Students swap the articles and impressions they found and thought up for homework. Students should attempt to answer their partner's question. After 5 minutes, students swap responses. Using the four key bullet points indicated in the top Examiner's tips box on page 35 of the Student Book, students peer-assess their partner's work, annotating it with positive comments. They then consider any bullet points not addressed by their partner or any overall target areas they could work on.

GradeStudio

Examiner tips
- Do not waste words or time. Every sentence should be making a point that will gain a tick.
- Follow the passage in a logical sequence. Go with the writer, taking the argument step by step and selecting relevant material.
- Use your own words where you can, but include plenty of evidence from the passage.
- Link your impressions to evidence from the passage.

2 Whole-class/paired work

Introduce Activity 1 on pages 34–35 of the Student Book. Students read the extract about the Duchess of Northumberland. Pairs then spend 1–2 minutes discussing their initial impressions of the Duchess.

Distribute **Worksheet 1.15**. Pairs find evidence to support the impressions identified in the table on the worksheet. After 10 minutes, ask pairs to consider what this table reinforces about how to approach 'What impressions?' questions – what steps must

they follow in order to answer these questions successfully? Take feedback, writing students' suggestions on the board.

Suggested answers for the table in **Worksheet 1.15** are provided in **Worksheet 1.16**.

Starter
- **Talk partners**: EAL students should be paired with a fluent English speaker to aid understanding by discussion of the assessment points.

Introduction/Whole-class work

Activity 1
- **Active listening**: teacher or fluent student readers should take turns to read part of the story using expression, pauses, facial expression and perhaps gestures to aid understanding. Clarify any difficult socio-cultural words with **message abundancy** such as 'Duchess', 'stronghold', 'driving force', 'hunch', 'foot and mouth crisis', 'dogged by', 'Geordie'…

- **ICT**: paired students should skim the text for words/expressions not understood and use an online dictionary to find meanings.
- If the EAL students have difficulty finding evidence for initial impressions, make cards out of suggested answers in the Teacher Guide and create a **matching activity**.

Activity 2
- Revise the technique of Point and Evidence with an Explanation which is linked to the question.
- Sentence starters and phrases for commenting could be added to a word wall. EAL students could select several to use in their assessed piece to give variety.

3 Independent work
Introduce Activity 2 on pages 36–37 of the Student Book. Students write their response to this question.

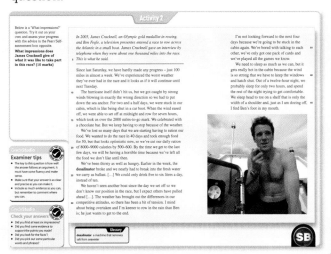

Suggested answers

Activity 1, pages 34–35   Activity 2, pages 36–37

4 Plenary
Ask students about James Cracknell's impressions of the race, and to give details from the text to support these impressions. Write their suggestions on the board.

Using this list and the Peer/Self-assessment box on page 37 of the Student Book, students self-assess their work. They then evaluate how successfully they addressed their own targets from the beginning of the lesson.

A table containing a number of different impressions is provided in **Worksheet 1.17**.

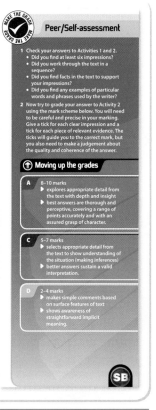

'Attitudes' questions
Teaching and learning and GradeStudio

Learning Objectives
- to understand how texts attempt to present a viewpoint or attitude towards their subject
- to develop an understanding of how to approach this type of question

Required resources
- Student Book, pages 38–41
- Worksheet 1.18: Understanding viewpoint and attitude
- Worksheet 1.19: What are Petronella's thoughts and feelings as she prepares to ride the TT course?
- Worksheet 1.20: what are Petronella's thoughts and feelings as she prepares to ride the TT course? – suggested answers

Assessment Objectives
Read and understand texts, selecting material appropriate to purpose, collating from different sources and making comparisons and cross-references as appropriate (English AO2i; English Language AO3i)

1 Starter
Use page 38 of the Student Book to remind students about viewpoint and attitude.

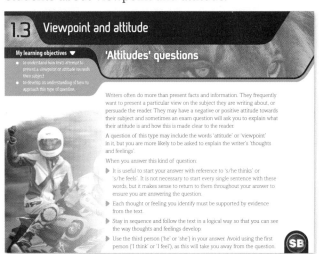

Distribute **Worksheet 1.18**. Explain that each of the statements on the worksheet expresses the speaker's thoughts and feelings. Ask students to consider what each statement tells the reader about the speaker's views and attitudes. Emphasise the range of information that can be gleaned.

Complete the first two statements as a whole class, taking feedback after each. Students complete the remaining three independently. Take feedback to ensure and consolidate understanding.

2 Whole-class work
Introduce Activity 1 on pages 38–39 of the Student Book and read the question and article. Distribute/display **Worksheet 1.19**, which contains the table for Activity 1. Introduce the first row, which has been completed, and ask students to consider whether the evidence is valid. Ask volunteers to explain *why*.

Students continue to explain the thoughts and feelings shown in the evidence selected from the article. After 10 minutes, students check their answers using the completed table on **Worksheet 1.20**. Students then use the completed table to write an answer to the exam question in Activity 1.

Starter activity
- When exploring viewpoint/attitude, thoughts/ feelings, and negative/positive, remind students that a single word ('disaster', 'joy'); short phrases using qualifiers ('no', 'most', 'too much', 'too little'), and prefixes ('**in**conceivable') inform the reader and can be used as evidence.
- Emphasise these with the first two examples in **Worksheet 1.19**. Model orally how to quote them in an exam question.

Whole-class work
- Share knowledge that may be new to some, e.g. 'Isle of Man', 'TT course' (Tourist Trophy course), 'ravine', 'pillion', 'scooters', 'leathers'. Footage may be found on YouTube.
- Read the text aloud. Intonation helps reveal thoughts/ feelings, aids finding evidence.

Independent work: explain socio-cultural idiomatic language ('mouth of death', 'jaws of Hell', 'hairpin bend', 'weedy') as evidence of thoughts, feelings and attitude.

Pair work
Mix a good language role model with an EAL learner.

3 Paired work

Turn to GradeStudio on pages 40–41 of the Student Book (sample answers C and A* with examiner comments). Note the examiner key points:
- the accuracy of reading
- the use of supporting evidence
- the focus on the question using key words (e.g. *feels* and *thinks*)
- the *range* of thoughts and feelings noted and discussed.

Once pairs have read the sample answers and examiner comments, they should summarise their findings in a lists of dos and don'ts for answers to 'attitudes' questions. Students should aim for three points for each.

4 Interactive GradeStudio

Open the interactive GradeStudio activity using ActiveTeach.

The objective of this activity is for students to understand the mark scheme.

Use this activity at the front of the class to assess sample answers at every grade, using the highlight tool and questions to assess the strengths and weaknesses of the answers.

Students put themselves in the position of the examiner and reward the sample answers with a grade.

5 Plenary

Give students 5 minutes to write a short guide to answering 'attitudes' questions. Students swap their guides with a partner. Have they included all the key points and features? Take feedback.

6 Further work

For homework, or in an IT suite or the school library, students select a newspaper or magazine article in which they feel the writer makes their viewpoint and attitude clear. Students then swap articles and write three or four paragraphs on how the writer does this.

Suggested answers

Starter
1 Suggests an adult speaker who makes broad judgements based on personal experience – and dislikes young people on the strength of it.

2 Suggests someone who values social skills more than, or at least as much as, a more formal, academic education; or perhaps a student who does not appreciate the value of homework!

3 Suggests someone who supports the political party currently in opposition.

4 Someone who believes everything they read and hear, perhaps an anxious or vulnerable person.

5 Someone who takes great pride in their appearance – or who was paid to endorse a product.

Activity 1, page 38
Suggested answers are provided on **Worksheet 1.20**.

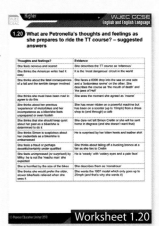

'Attitudes' questions
Exam practice and assessment

Learning Objectives
- to practise 'attitudes' questions
- to develop an understanding of how to approach this type of question

Required resources
- Student Book, pages 42–43
- Video clip 1.3: *Newsround Extra*
- Worksheet 1.21: What's the viewpoint?
- Worksheet 1.22: Viewpoint and attitude questions – the weak response
- Worksheet 1.23: What are Bill Bryson's thoughts and feelings about Blackpool? – suggested answers

Assessment Objectives
Read and understand texts, selecting material appropriate to purpose, collating from different sources and making comparisons and cross-references as appropriate (English AO2i; English Language AO3i)

1 Starter

Write the words 'viewpoint' and 'attitude' on the board. Ask students what they understand by these terms. Encourage and note a range of responses on the board. Aim to define the relationship between viewpoint and opinion: viewpoint is the writer/speaker's broad opinion on a particular topic which will be supported with a range of specific opinions.

Introduce **Video clip 1.3**: an extract from *Newsround Extra* on landfill and recycling.

Video 1.3

Display/distribute **Worksheet 1.21**. Ask students to watch the video clip to establish their understanding of content, then watch it again, noting on the worksheet the reporter's viewpoint and the clues they used to identify it. Take feedback, encouraging a range of responses.

Worksheet 1.21

Create a checklist on the board of the key clues that can help us identify a writer's viewpoint and attitude, for example: the use of carefully selected images; use of facts/statistics (e.g. every year each household produces one ton of waste...); choice of language ('piles up... dumped... never rot away...').

2 Whole-class/paired work

Read the introduction and the examiner tips on page 42 of the Student Book. Introduce Activity 1 and read the question and the Bryson extract about Blackpool.

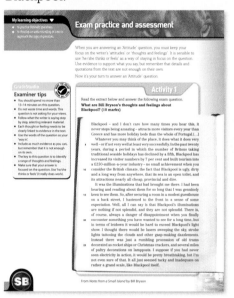

Distribute **Worksheet 1.22**, which contains a number of sample responses to Activity 1. Use the worksheet to explain the task. Students complete the task in pairs. After 5 minutes, take feedback, encouraging students to make the connection between the problem and the correct examiner tip.

Suggested answers are provided in the 'Suggested answers' box opposite.

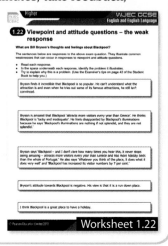

Worksheet 1.22

Starter
- **Talk partners** discuss worksheet 1.21 'What's the viewpoint?'.
- **Whole class/paired work**: use 'Examiner tips' on page 42 of the Student Book, to aid understanding particularly of 'relevant'. Remind students about Point Evidence Explain (P.E.E.).
- The checklist could be added to the **word wall**.

N.B. Worksheet 1.22 is especially helpful for EAL students.

Independent work/Activity 3
- **Active listening**: Read the text aloud using expression, pauses, facial expression and gesture to aid understanding.
- Use **message abundancy** to assemble and clarify

vocabulary and words Bryson uses to paint a disparaging view of Blackpool.
- **ICT-based tools**: E-thesaurus and dictionaries could also be helpful but be aware that EAL students may have difficulty in selecting the correct words for the context.
- Create **substitution tables** to practice openers such as: He thinks /feels /says /expresses the view that.

Plenary
- Cut up copies of Worksheet 1.23 and use as **matching activity**.
- **Clarify** as appropriate words in 'Moving up the grades' e.g. 'perceptive', 'accurately', 'valid'.

3 Independent work

Students produce a response to the question: What are Bill Bryson's thoughts and feelings about Blackpool? Ask students to then use step 1 of the Peer/Self-assessment section on page 43 of the Student Book to check their answers.

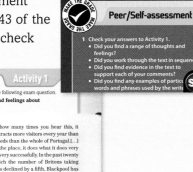

Suggested answers

Suggested answers for Worksheet 1.22

1st response: No quotations are used here to support the points being made.

2nd response: Though there are comments and quotations used, there is no explanation of how Bryson's thoughts and feelings are made clear to us, or why Bryson has these particular thoughts and feelings about Blackpool.

3rd response: This answer relies solely on quotations doing all of the work – there is no student commentary to explain what the quotations suggest or show us about Bryson's thoughts and feelings.

4th response: This answer is too broad and unspecific. It is a summative answer rather than one that will encourage close analysis of the whole extract.

5th response: This is irrelevant – the question does not ask for personal opinion of Blackpool.

Activity 1, page 42

Suggested answers are provided on **Worksheet 1.23**.

4 Plenary

Using ActiveTeach, display **Worksheet 1.23**. Students swap responses with a partner and assess their partner's work by checking it against the worksheet.

Next, students mark their partner's work using step 2 of the Peer/Self-assessment section on page 43 of the Student Book.

Students return their partner's work and feed back their comments to each other.

Ask: What are the key ingredients of a successful viewpoint and attitude response? Create a class checklist on the board.

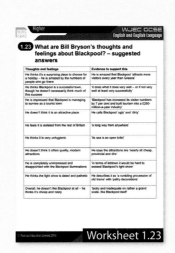

'Intended audience' questions
Teaching and learning

Learning Objectives
- to understand how texts target particular individuals or groups of people
- to learn how to approach this type of question

Assessment Objectives
Read and understand texts, selecting material appropriate to purpose, collating from different sources and making comparisons and cross-references as appropriate (English AO2i; English Language AO3i)

Required resources
- Student Book, pages 44–47
- Video clip 1.4: *Strictly Come Dancing*
- Video clip 1.5: *Newsnight*
- Worksheet 1.24: Who is the intended audience?

1 Starter

Students explain what they understand by the phrase 'target audience'. Encourage a range of responses.

Introduce the video clips by asking students to think about who is being targeted in each clip, and how they are being targeted. Ask: How can we tell who the target audience is?

Distribute **Worksheet 1.24** and explain the task. Watch the video clips. Students make notes independently as they watch each clip.

Ask: Who was the intended audience in each clip and how did we know? Take feedback, encouraging full responses.

Ask: What choices can writers make to target a specific audience?

Create a class checklist on the board, using students' suggestions.

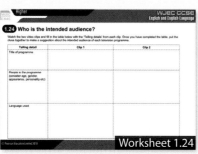

2 Whole-class/paired work

Introduce page 44 of the Student Book and explain the Learning Objectives.

As a class, read the text about Connaught Gardens on page 45. Students identify any choices from the class checklist (compiled in the Starter activity) that the writer has made to target a specific audience.

In pairs, students spend 10 minutes answering the questions in Activity 1 on page 44 of the Student Book. Model how to use the answers from this activity to write the beginning of an exam-style response to the question 'Who is this leaflet trying to attract to the Connaught Gardens?' Remind students to use the wording of the question to start the answer, and then the ideas highlighted in the questions in Activity 1, combined with their responses to those questions, to formulate the answer, e.g. *The sub-heading 'step back in time' and enjoy 'tranquil surroundings' makes it clear that the leaflet is aimed at … because … tend to appeal to them…*. Students complete this response in pairs.

3 Independent work

Introduce the advert for Llandudno on page 47 of the Student Book. Students read it independently and identify which features of the text they would focus on to explain its intended audience. Take feedback, encouraging developed responses.

Students complete Activity 2 on page 46.

4 Plenary

Look back at the class checklist from the Starter. Based on today's learning, ask students to suggest any additional choices that should be added to the list.

Students evaluate the impact of these choices on making the intended audience clear, then write out the choices in rank order. Explain that learning this checklist will help to ensure effective reading in the exam.

5 Further work

For homework, students find a leaflet for a local attraction or place of interest. They should identify on the leaflet the key clues that make the intended audience clear. Students then devise a series of questions like those in Activities 1 and 2 that would guide a peer to understanding the intended audience of the text.

Suggested answers

Activity 2, page 46

1 • Paddling in the water, playing the sands, children's play area, wonderful views, Punch and Judy (pictured), donkey rides (pictured), organised games, stalls and amusements, supervised activities for children, paddling pool.
  • 'halcyon days' suggests parents will be creating happy memories for their children
    Choice of two beaches: 'quieter ... lively' suggests something for everyone
    Positive language: 'wonderful... popularity... famed... toddlers love...'

2 These activities are of more interest to parents than their children.

3 This is aimed at people who are looking for a more active holiday. The activities such as 'angling, riding, windsurfing' and language, e.g. 'energetic...' reinforce this.

4 This section is largely intended to appeal to anglers. It provides contact details and some information to show that all aspects of fishing are catered for.

'Intended audience' questions
GradeStudio and Assessment

Learning Objectives
- to practise questions about 'Intended audience'
- to develop a clear understanding of what is required by this type of question

Required resources
- Student Book, pages 48–51
- Worksheet 1.25: Llandudno sample answer
- Worksheet 1.25a: Llandudno sample answer – suggested answers
- Worksheet 1.26: Blackpool Zoo sample answers

Assessment Objectives
Read and understand texts, selecting material appropriate to purpose, collating from different sources and making comparisons and cross-references as appropriate (English AO2i; English Language AO3i)

1 Starter

Display/distribute **Worksheet 1.25** and explain the task. The worksheet contains the D grade answer from page 48 of the Student Book. In pairs, students explain each area of weakness in the sample answer. After 5 minutes take feedback, using students' ideas to annotate the answer on the whiteboard.

Students consider what this answer has shown them about things to avoid when producing answers to 'Intended audience' questions. Take feedback.

Suggested answers are provided on **Worksheet 1.25a**.

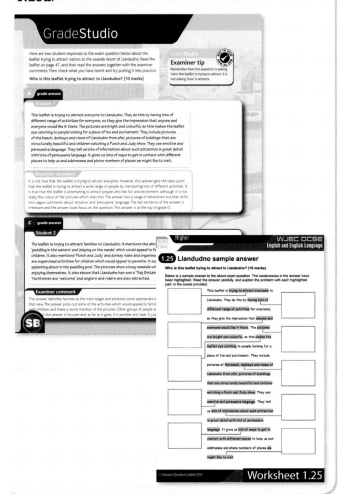

2 Whole-class/paired work

Look at pages 48–49 of the Student Book to establish the examiner comments and tips on how to improve.

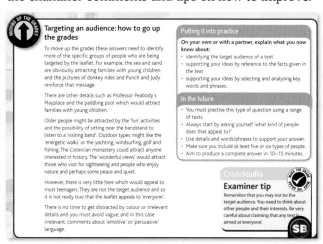

Using the examiner tips, students work in pairs to improve the sample answer on **Worksheet 1.25**. After 10 minutes, partners swap their improved responses and assess each other's work, evaluating the success of each improvement and deciding whether the answer has moved up a grade.

Students feed back their comments to each other and suggest a target area to work on.

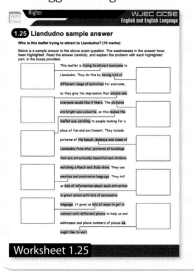

Starter
- **Talk partners**: pair an EAL learner with a fluent English speaker to discuss the original text on page 46 of the Student Book.
- **Message abundancy**: check students' understanding of the examiner tips on page 48.

N.B
- It is important to draw attention to what the question is asking as EAL students often misread questions.
- Encourage them to give specific evidence.

- Timing is also important as it is common for EAL students to 'run out of time'.

Activity 5
- **Active reading**: choose fluent readers to read chunks of text – EAL students could have difficulty with pronunciation which would hinder understanding: 'browsing', 'miniature', 'invertebrates'…
- Use a **mind map** or **spider diagram** to link the activities offered to specific age groups to answer the question 'Who is the leaflet aimed at?'
- Clarify difficult words in the assessment list on page 51
- Use one of the sample zoo answers in the worksheet to create a **dictogloss** which peers will assess.

3 Independent work
Introduce Activity 1 on pages 50–51 of the Student Book. Students answer the question.

4 Plenary
Distribute copies of **Worksheet 1.26** to pairs. The worksheet contains three sample answers. Explain that, using both the mark scheme provided on page 51 of the Student Book and their knowledge of strong and weak exam answers, students should rank the answers and establish which is grade D, C and A. (Sample answer 1 = D; Sample answer 2 = A; Sample answer 3 = C). Take feedback to ensure understanding.

In each answer, students identify phrases that make the grade clear, e.g. for the D answer, an example of 'simple comments based on surface features of text'. Take feedback to establish clear examples with the class.

Students self-assess their answers to Activity 1 and reflect on a key target to help them improve.

Suggested answers

Suggested answers for Worksheet 1.25
Suggested answers are provided on Worksheet 1.25a.

Activity 1, pages 50–51
- This leaflet is primarily trying to attract families to Blackpool Zoo.
- The very first sentence on the leaflet is 'Blackpool Zoo really is a day out for all the family'.
- This statement is then quickly supported with the mention of the 'family restaurant' and 'miniature railway', both of which make the zoo sound like it has been designed for the needs of a young family.
- There is also recognition that parents, and perhaps grandparents, may want to do something other than look at animals all day, with the mention of the 'quality gift shops' and the 'coffee shop'.
- The pictures of young children looking happy, interested and entertained reinforce that the zoo is child-friendly.
- It is clear that there are plenty of fun things for children to do – there is a 'play zone' and a chance to watch 'animal feeds'; children can have their faces painted or handle one of the animals.
- Moreover, the leaflet makes it clear that visiting the zoo also has educational benefits – not only is the 'fantastic education team' mentioned, but the numerous exotic animals that the zoo houses are listed.
- In this section, the words 'safe, open spaces', 'play areas' and 'natural enclosures' again reinforce the child-friendly quality of the zoo.
- Finally, it is obvious that the zoo takes conservation very seriously, so the leaflet could also be aimed at environmentally aware people who take an interest in animal conservation.
- The leaflet mentions that the zoo is 'a great supporter of conservation projects around the world', which could encourage people to visit the zoo to show their support for this cause.

Persuasive techniques
Teaching and learning

Learning Objectives
- to understand the techniques writers use to influence readers
- to learn how to approach this type of question

Required resources
- Student Book, pages 52–53
- Worksheet 1.27: WWF leaflet
- Worksheet 1.28: Persuasive techniques: what to consider
- Worksheet 1.29: Persuasive techniques: what to consider – suggested answers

Assessment Objectives
Read and understand texts, selecting material appropriate to purpose, collating from different sources and making comparisons and cross-references as appropriate (English AO2i; English Language AO3i)

1 Starter

Distribute copies of **Worksheet 1.27**. Explain that this leaflet is trying to persuade readers to adopt a tiger. In pairs, students identify the different ways WWF have tried to persuade readers to sign up to this scheme.

Students annotate their copies of the worksheet with their ideas. After 5 minutes, take feedback, encouraging a range of ideas to illustrate the range of techniques used.

Worksheet 1.27

2 Whole-class/paired work

Using page 52 of the Student Book, introduce the section on persuasive techniques.

Distribute copies of **Worksheet 1.28**. Students discuss in pairs, and record individually, what they understand each point on the persuasive techniques checklist to mean.

Students then find examples of each aspect in the WWF leaflet on **Worksheet 1.27**.

After 15 minutes, take feedback to consolidate and ensure understanding.

A completed version of the table on **Worksheet 1.28** is available on **Worksheet 1.29**.

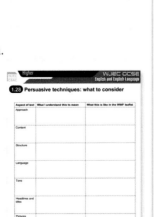
Worksheet 1.28

3 Independent work

Using ActiveTeach, display the article about Katherine Legge and read it with the whole class.

Look at the first annotated feature in the text. Ask: Why is this persuasive, and which aspect of persuasive techniques is it an example of?

Write students' ideas on the board; students should also note these down.

Students continue with this exercise independently, explaining which aspect of persuasive techniques each annotated feature is an example of.

Starter
- **ICT-based tools**: It could be useful to explore the meaning of 'persuade', 'persuasion', 'persuasive' using an online dictionary and thesaurus.

Activity 1
- **Active listening**: the teacher or fluent class readers should read the texts aloud using clear expression, pauses, gestures and facial expression to facilitate understanding - the repressed emotion of the firefighter; the manic excitement of Petronella and the mad danger of Hunn.

- **Highlight** examples of the different techniques in the texts.
- **Page 72**: clarify socio-cultural, idiomatic and technical language: e.g. 'fire within', 'instincts', 'yobs', 'intercept', '£30K', 'drunk'.
- **Page 76**: clarify socio-cultural, idiomatic and technical language: e.g. 'gargantuan', 'pillion seat', 'revs up', 'opens the throttle', 'higher than a kite', 'to black out'.
- Use the 'Putting into practice' and 'In the future' sections on page 81 as short **dictogloss** activities – as an aide memoire.
- **Page 80-1**: Remind the students of the P.E.E. technique.

4 Plenary

Look back at the question in Activity 1 on page 52 of the Student Book.

> ### Activity 1
>
> The extract opposite by Fabienne Williams is about a racing driver called Katherine Legge. The annotations are in response to the following question:
>
> **How does the writer try to show the reader that Katherine Legge is a serious and talented racing driver? (10 marks)**
>
> Use the annotated text to produce an answer to this question in no more than fifteen minutes.
>
>

Model how to start the answer to this question: remind students to use the wording of the question to begin, and then to use the text annotation and their own explanations about which aspect of persuasive text each annotation illustrates, to develop their response, e.g. *'Fabienne Williams' approach in this article is to begin by admitting that not many people outside the USA have seen Katherine Legge race…'*.

Allocate the remaining features from the text to pairs of students so that each pair has one part of the text to focus on. On displayable paper, pairs answer the question with a sentence that focuses on their allocated part of the text.

After 5 minutes, pairs stick their sentences to the board in an appropriate sequence to create a full answer. Ask students to evaluate the strengths and weaknesses in the answer, and what this shows them about how to approach this sort of task.

5 Further work

For homework, students find another example of a real-life persuasive text, trying to find one that incorporates all eight aspects. Students identify these aspects by annotating the text. This will serve as a useful revision tool.

Suggested answers

Suggested answers to **Worksheet 1.28** are provided in **Worksheet 1.29**.

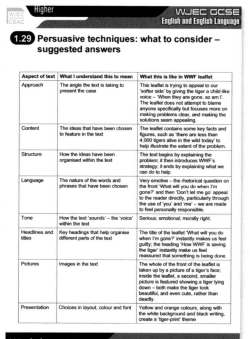

Worksheet 1.29

Persuasive approaches
Teaching and learning

Learning Objectives

- to understand how an underlying approach influences the reader
- to gain an overview of persuasive tactics

Required resources

- Student Book, pages 54–55
- Worksheet 1.30: How to persuade
- Worksheet 1.31: Persuasive approaches
- Worksheet 1.32: Persuasive approaches – suggested answers

Assessment Objectives

Read and understand texts, selecting material appropriate to purpose, collating from different sources and making comparisons and cross-references as appropriate (English AO2i; English Language AO3i)

1 Starter

Distribute copies of **Worksheet 1.30** and explain the task. Independently or in pairs, students come up with as many different ways of persuading the person to stop smoking as possible. After 5–7 minutes, take feedback. Encourage students to identify techniques their peers have made use of.

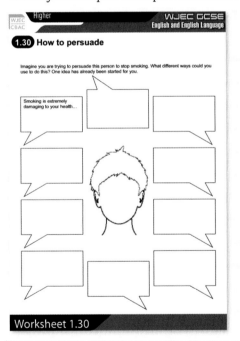

2 Whole-class/paired work

Using page 54 of the Student Book, introduce the idea of a 'persuasive approach'.

Using the explanations of the different categories of 'approach', students identify which approaches they used on **Worksheet 1.30**.

Once they have identified the approaches they had already considered, students should add additional speech bubbles to their sheets for approaches they had not yet used. After 10 minutes, take feedback to consolidate and ensure understanding of these key approaches.

Starter
- **Talk partners**: pair an EAL student with a fluent English student to discuss and clarify the list of emotional responses: 'scare tactics', 'shock', 'appeal' (including the explanations such as 'insecurities', 'outrage', 'sensational', 'vanity', 'snobbery'. **Message abundancy** could be used in a whole-class discussion afterwards.
- **Writing frames** could be created as a scaffold for writing the different kinds of 'argument' listed on page 54 of the Student Book.

Activity 1
- Before reading the text on page 55, **activate prior knowledge** of food vocabulary by discussing what students eat for school lunch.
- **Active reading**: the teacher or a series of fluent readers should read the text carefully trying to convey the tone used. Alternatively, groups could experiment with reading in different tones. Clarify, as appropriate, any unknown vocabulary, e.g. 'greaseburger', 'deep-fried delicacy', spaghetti bolognese', 'we shrug our shoulders', 'artery-clogging', 'marketing ploy'.

3 Independent work
Turn to page 55 of the Student Book and introduce Activity 1.

Distribute copies of **Worksheet 1.31**. Students identify examples of different approaches from the article, completing the table on the worksheet accordingly.

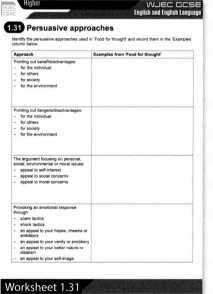

4 Plenary
Ask: What is the most significant/prominent approach that has been taken in the 'Food for thought' extract?

Students consider, and make a note or diagram (e.g. mind map) to show when certain approaches might be favoured, and which approaches are most likely to be used together.

5 Further work
For homework, students find examples of real-life persuasive texts that demonstrate the range of approaches that can be taken.

Suggested answers

Activity 1, page 55
Suggested answers are shown on **Worksheet 1.32**.

Persuasive content
Teaching and learning and GradeStudio

Learning Objective
- to learn how writers use content to influence readers

Required resources
- Student Book, pages 56–59
- Worksheet 1.33: Key aspects of persuasive content – card sort
- Worksheet 1.34: How does the writer try to suggest that parents are as bad as teenagers?
- Worksheet 1.35: How does the writer try to suggest that parents are as bad as teenagers? – suggested answers

- Worksheet 1.36: What mark would these student achieve?
- Worksheet 1.36a: What mark would these students achieve? – suggested answers.
- Worksheet 1.37: Improving a response

Assessment Objectives
Read and understand texts, selecting material appropriate to purpose, collating from different sources and making comparisons and cross-references as appropriate (English AO2i; English Language AO3i)

1 Starter

Distribute copies of **Worksheet 1.33** to pairs and allow them 5 minutes to try to match each 'aspect of content' with the correct 'explanation' and 'effect this has on argue/persuade writing'. Take feedback to ensure students have the correct answers.

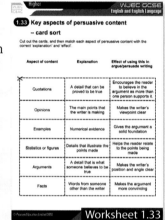

2 Whole-class/paired work

Turn to page 56 of the Student Book to reinforce the idea of 'Persuasive content'.

Using ActiveTeach, display the article 'Who's the real Kevin?' for Activity 1. Zoom in on the article so that the analysis comments are not displayed.

Distribute copies of **Worksheet 1.34**. Pairs identify how the writer tries to suggest that parents are as bad as teenagers. They should select evidence from the text, then identify what aspect of persuasive content it is.

After 10 minutes, give students the chance to compare their ideas with the points on page 56. A full range of suggested answers are provided on **Worksheet 1.35**. Ask: What aspect of persuasive content has this writer used the most to make the article convincing?

Emphasise to students that for an exam question focusing on persuasive content, it is the specific answers from the text that matter more than the 'feature spotting'.

3 GradeStudio

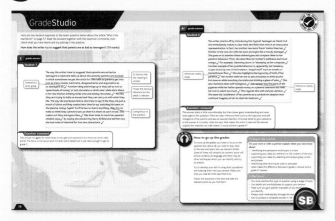

Turn to page 58 of the Student Book and introduce the exam question. With the class, read Student 1 and Student 2's responses, as well as the examiner comments.

Using the understanding gained from this, students work in pairs to create a mini-mark scheme to reflect what they feel examiners are looking for at grades A* down to C.

After 5 minutes, pairs feed back key ideas.

Establish an agreed class mark scheme and write it on the board; students make a note of this too.

Distribute copies of **Worksheet 1.36**, which contains two additional student responses. Students try to mark the two responses.

Suggested answers are provided on **Worksheet 1.36a**.

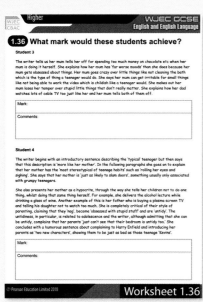

Worksheet 1.36

4 Plenary

Distribute copies of **Worksheet 1.37**, which contains the student response from page 58 of the Student Book. Using their understanding of good answers, students attempt to improve this response.

After 5 minutes, students swap responses and peer-assess, again using the agreed class mark scheme. Partners feed back their comments to each other.

Students sum up their understanding of how to write about persuasive content in three bullet points.

Worksheet 1.37

5 Further work

For homework, students find a persuasive text that has influenced them.

Suggested answers

Activity 1, page 56

Suggested answers are shown on **Worksheet 1.35**.

Suggested answers for Worksheet 1.36

Suggested answers are provided on **Worksheet 1.36**.

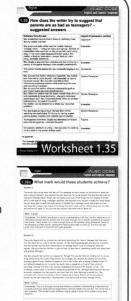

Worksheet 1.35

Worksheet 1.36a

Persuasive structure

Teaching and learning

Learning Objectives
- to understand what is meant by the structure of a text
- to understand how writers use structure to influence readers

Required resources
- Student Book, pages 60–61
- Worksheet 1.38: Persuasive structure
- Worksheet 1.39: Alzheimer's Research Trust Leaflet
- Worksheet 1.40: Steps in the argument cards
- Worksheet 1.41: Typical structural choices in a persuasive text
- Worksheet 1.41a: Typical structural choices in a persuasive text – Suggested answers

Assessment Objectives
Read and understand texts, selecting material appropriate to purpose, collating from different sources and making comparisons and cross-references as appropriate (English AO2i; English Language AO3i)

1 Starter

Distribute copies of **Worksheet 1.38**, which contains text from a leaflet that has been jumbled in the wrong order. Read the instructions at the top of the worksheet. Students carry out the task. After 5–7 minutes, display the original leaflet on **Worksheet 1.39** to allow students to check their answers, sticking down the paragraphs in the right order.

Students describe what each paragraph is about and what it is trying to achieve: In what way is it persuasive?

Ask: Why has the text been organised in this way? Take feedback to ensure and consolidate understanding.

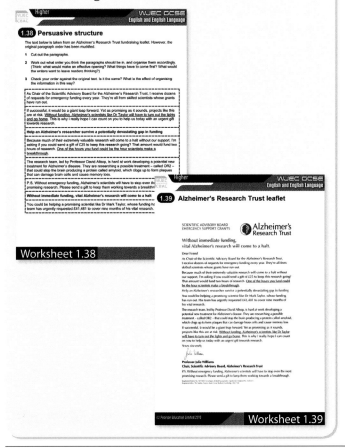

2 Whole-class/paired work

Turn to page 60 of the Student Book to explain the concept of structure in texts, and how it is another technique that writers use to influence readers.

Using ActiveTeach, display the Oxfam advertisement on page 61. Cut out the 'steps in the argument' cards from **Worksheet 1.40** and distribute them around the room.

Read the Oxfam advertisement with the class. As students identify the 'step in the argument' in the text that is on their card, they stick their card to the whiteboard.

Once all cards are on the whiteboard, give pairs 2 minutes to discuss the impact of the way this text has been organised. Take feedback to consolidate and ensure understanding.

Turn to page 60 of the Student Book and introduce task 3 of Activity 1. In pairs, students follow the instructions to identify the steps in the argument in the 'Who's the Real Kevin?' text on page 57. After 10 minutes take feedback, writing students' responses on the whiteboard, next to the 'steps in the argument' cards for the Oxfam advertisement.

Students consider any similarities between the steps in the arguments in the two texts.

EAL additional support

Starter

- **Talk partners**: pair a fluent English speaker with an EAL student to work together to ensure understanding of the instructions for the persuasive structure **sequencing** activity.
- It could be useful to pair EAL students with the same first language as a way of **activating prior knowledge**. They could discuss some charities that work in their home countries in their L1 and share their knowledge in a whole-class discussion.

Activity 1

- **Active listening**: read around the class to aid understanding and pronunciation of both the Oxfam text on page 61 and the list of comments on structure on page 60. Be prepared to **clarify** any difficult cultural or idiomatic words and phrases such as: 'comfortable lifestyle', 'moral injustice', 'mosquito', 'malaria', 'cholera', 'diarrhoea', 'midwife'.

3 Independent work

Look again at the Alzheimer's Research Trust text on **Worksheet 1.39**. Students identify the 'steps' in the argument in this text. They are now evaluating how the argument has been developed.

4 Plenary

Considering all three texts from today's lesson, students reflect on typical features of the structure of a persuasive text.

Distribute copies of **Worksheet 1.41** and use the instructions on the worksheet to explain the task. After 5 minutes, take feedback to consolidate and ensure understanding. Suggested answers are provided on **Worksheet 1.41a**.

Suggested answers

Activity 3, Task 1, page 60

- The writer's mother is more like Harry Enfield's character than the writer is.
- Her mother behaves like a teenager when she is annoyed.
- She does exactly what she tells her daughter not to do.
- She is frequently irritable and over-reacts to problems.
- She does not think her daughter can organise her own life.
- The writer's father is just as bad: he is a hypocrite too.
- The writer admits she spends too much money: she is not perfect.
- Her parents are just as untidy as she is.
- Teenagers are not fairly represented in the media: parents are just as bad.

Suggested answers for Worksheet 1.41

Suggested answers are provided on **Worksheet 1.41a**.

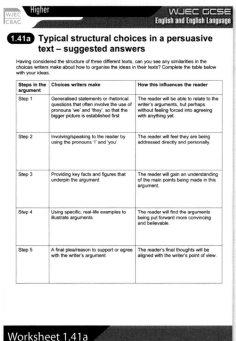

Language used to influence
Teaching and learning

Learning Objective
- to understand how writers use language to influence and persuade

Required resources
- Student Book, pages 62–65
- Worksheet 1.39: Alzheimer's Research Trust Leaflet
- Worksheet 1.42: How can language influence us?
- Past exam papers

Assessment Objectives
Read and understand texts, selecting material appropriate to purpose, collating from different sources and making comparisons and cross-references as appropriate (English AO2i; English Language AO3i)

1 Starter

Distribute copies of **Worksheet 1.42**. Students locate the text from the Alzheimer's Research Trust leaflet which they looked at on **Worksheet 1.39**. Read the instructions at the top of Worksheet 1.42. Students carry out the task. After 5 minutes, take feedback, including any additional examples students have managed to find in the text.

Ask: What different things can influence us and persuade us to act, for example 'guilt'? Write students' ideas on the board.

Make the point that language in persuasive texts will harness the power of those influential forces.

2 Whole-class/paired work

Turn to page 62 of the Student Book and introduce Activity 1. Read the article as a class.

Students work in pairs to complete task 2 of Activity 1.

Take feedback to consolidate and ensure understanding.

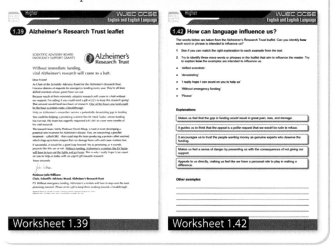

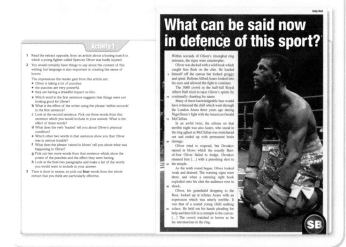

Starter
- Use **talk partners** to clarify 'Alzheimer's', 'devastating', 'consequences'.
- **ICT-based tools**: use online dictionaries and thesaurus to explore differences between 'persuade' and 'influence'. Also explore other words from the same root word which could be useful for answering exam questions: e.g. 'influence', 'influential', 'influencing' and 'persuasive', 'persuade', 'persuasion'.

Activities 1 and 2
- **Active listening**: the texts on pages 63-64 of the Student Book should be read aloud by the teacher and fluent readers with expression, pauses, facial expression and gestures to aid understanding as well as the selection of evidence.
- Some EAL learners may need more clarification of technical, socio-cultural and idiomatic vocabulary, e.g. <u>multiple meanings</u>: 'decked', 'hook', 'flush', 'groggy', 'spent', 'temple'.
  <u>idiomatic</u>: 'rained in', 'fleet-of-foot', 'awful twist', 'machismo', 'cut down', 'on hand'.
- Teach strategies for decoding and deciphering.
- Make a **word wall** of adjectives and adverbs which express/influence opinions.

3 Independent work
Students read the second article about Spencer Oliver on page 64 of the Student Book, then complete Activity 2 on page 65.

4 Plenary
Look at some past exam papers and ask students to identify questions that require comment on 'language used to influence'. Students identify the common features of these questions.

Students write a 'language used to influence' exam-style question for each of the three texts they have explored today.

Students consider what they should include in a checklist on how to answer a 'language used to influence' question. Take feedback and establish a class checklist.

5 Further work
Students swap the exam questions they generated in the Plenary. For homework, they write an answer to one of the questions.

Suggested answers

Activity 1, page 62
2 a catastrophic
  b it shows how quickly things went wrong
  c decked, wild, flush – all show the power and accuracy of the punches
  d he was exhausted/badly hurt
  e groggy and spent
  f he was taking a lot of punches and he could not avoid them
  g stunned, punishing
  h weak, drained, stunning, exploded, shock, terrible, scared, child, solace, pleading, crumple, horror, unconscious

3 any sensible selection

Activity 2, page 65
1 vehemently

2 it makes it seem uncivilised or inhuman

3 it is wrong and it does not help society and so cannot be 'justified' in those terms

4 gratuitous

5 they are pumped up with male aggression

6 abhorrent, despicable

7 bloodthirsty, cruel

8 unholy

Persuasive tone
Teaching and Learning

Learning Objective
- to understand how writers use tone to influence readers

Required resources
- Student Book, pages 66–67
- Worksheet 1.43: Tone words
- Worksheet 1.44: What's the tone?
- Worksheet 1.45: Tone in different pieces of writing

Assessment Objectives
Read and understand texts, selecting material appropriate to purpose, collating from different sources and making comparisons and cross-references as appropriate (English AO2i; English Language AO3i)

1 Starter

Distribute copies of **Worksheet 1.43**, which contains the tone words from Activity 1 on page 66 of the Student Book. Students define each of the tone words, completing the table on the worksheet in pairs. They may need dictionaries.

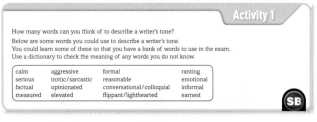

2 Whole-class/paired work

Tone

Tone is the way something is said or written, or the manner in which the reader is addressed. Writers adopt various tones, just as we do in speech, depending on whom they are addressing and what they are trying to achieve. Most of us learn at an early age how to use tone to try to get what we want!

Think about the question 'Please can I have…?' How exactly would you say this? Your answer means that you are beginning to understand tone.

Similarly, if you fall off your chair in class, the teacher may say: 'Well, that was clever.' The meaning is the exact opposite of the literal meaning of the words. The sarcasm is achieved through tone.

When you are reading, think about the tone the writer adopts and the reason for it. There is a contrast between texts that want to seem factual and reasonable and those that are expressing strong feelings. Writers may take the emotional heat out of an issue (usually if they writing a defensive piece). Others may seek as much emotional impact as possible. Occasionally, these can be fiercely one-sided, making no attempt to be balanced.

Use page 66 of the Student Book to introduce what 'tone' is in writing. Distribute mini-whiteboards to pairs.

Explain the task for **Worksheet 1.44** using the instructions provided. Display the sentences on the worksheet, one at a time. For each sentence, allow pairs 2 minutes to discuss the tone, the words that make the tone clear and how tone could influence the reader.

Pairs record their answers on mini-whiteboards.

See mini-whiteboard responses for each sentence.

Starter
- **Active listening**: read the explanation of tone on page 66 as a class. Students should note the words they do not understand. Use **message abundancy** to clarify vocabulary as appropriate.
- EAL students who share an L1 could discuss the concept of 'tone' in their L1 to aid understanding.
- Bilingual dictionaries and online resources may be useful for completing Worksheets 1.43 and 1.44.
- **Matching activity**: make cards with the tone words

and ask the students to make pairs of opposites where possible e.g. 'measured' 'ranting'.

Independent work/Activity 2
- Add the tone words on page 66 to a **word wall**.
- **Active listening**: read aloud the extracts on page 67 of the Student Book (or use fluent readers) with expression, pauses, facial expression and gestures to aid understanding as well as the selection of evidence. Give the students **visual approaches**, such as a red card to raise whenever they hear words they don't understand. Clarify.
- **Text highlighting** could be done on the worksheet as you read.

3 Independent work

Turn to page 66 in the Student Book and introduce Activity 2.

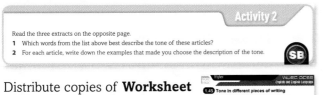

Activity 2

Read the three extracts on the opposite page.
1 Which words from the list above best describe the tone of these articles?
2 For each article, write down the examples that made you choose the description of the tone.

Distribute copies of **Worksheet 1.45**. Students read the three extracts on page 67, and complete the worksheet with their ideas.

Worksheet 1.45

4 Plenary

Students list the different kinds of persuasive texts that exist (e.g. charity campaign material, holiday brochure). Beside each item, students identify the sort of tone that would be most likely to help the text achieve its purpose. After 5 minutes, take feedback to share ideas and consolidate learning.

Suggested answers

Activities 2 and 3, page 67

Extract	Words to describe tone	Words from the extract that create this tone	How this influences the readers
1	ironic/sarcastic light-hearted	'festival of litter' 'citizens had taken time off' 'to the otherwise bland and neglected landscape' 'They fluttered gaily in the bushes' 'And to think that elsewhere …'	The light-hearted but sarcastic tone used here will make the reader laugh, and in doing so will emphasise the absurdity of littering.
2	informal conversational	'It has all sorts of nasty connotations' 'Well, surprisingly, exercise does not have to be this way' 'It can be enjoyable' 'You don't even have to leave the comfort…' 'Intrigued?' '… all it really means is that you don't have to end up panting'	The writer uses an informal and conversational tone to establish familiarity with the reader, thereby getting the reader on board with their point of view.
3	opinionated sarcastic conversational	'It is also, I would add, one of the most ugly' 'The faint odour of Thatcherite depression' 'For all those people who wish to have their romantic image of Suffolk … shattered, Lowestoft is the place to go' 'The seafront reeks of greasy fish and chips' 'Please excuse my faintly incredulous tone'	This piece is very opinionated, and many of the writer's opinions are written as though they are facts. This strongly opinionated tone, coupled with sarcasm and a conversational element, makes the writer's viewpoint very convincing. It would be hard for the reader to disagree.

Persuasive headlines and titles
Teaching and learning

Learning Objective
- to understand how headlines and titles influence readers

Required resources
- Student Book, pages 68–69
- Worksheet 1.46: Headlines
- Worksheet 1.47: Writing about headlines
- Worksheet 1.48: Analysing headlines
- Worksheet 1.49: Analysing headlines – suggested answers
- Worksheet 1.50: Writing about headlines: turning your analysis into an exam-style response

Assessment Objectives
Read and understand texts, selecting material appropriate to purpose, collating from different sources and making comparisons and cross-references as appropriate (English AO2i; English Language AO3i)

1 Starter

Distribute copies of **Worksheet 1.46**, which introduces students to the techniques used in headlines. Read the information and instructions at the top of the page. Students complete the tasks in pairs.

Hear students' own headlines. Students suggest which techniques their peers have used, and what their headlines are designed to achieve.

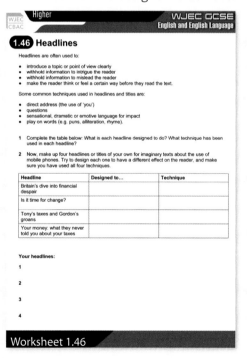

Worksheet 1.46

2 Whole-class work

Use page 68 of the Student Book to emphasise the importance of making commentary on headlines meaningful. Distribute copies of **Worksheet 1.47**.

PLEASE WILL YOU STOP PAYING TO HAVE MY PEOPLE MURDERED?

Using ActiveTeach, display the Friends of the Earth headline.

Students identify the techniques used in this headline, and what they feel it is designed to do. Annotate the headline with the students' ideas. Students record these on their worksheets.

Worksheet 1.47

Using ActiveTeach, display Student 1's response from page 68 of the Student Book. Give students 2 minutes to assess this response. Take feedback and annotate the response with students' ideas.

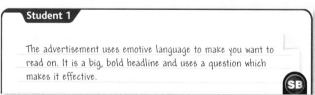

Student 1

The advertisement uses emotive language to make you want to read on. It is a big, bold headline and uses a question which makes it effective.

Students write an improved response in the space on their worksheets, then compare their improved responses with the Student 2 response on page 69.

Students consolidate their understanding of how to write about headlines and titles into a checklist.

3 Independent/paired work

Turn to page 69 in the Student Book and introduce Activity 1. Distribute copies of **Worksheet 1.48** for students to record their answers, and display the same worksheet using ActiveTeach.

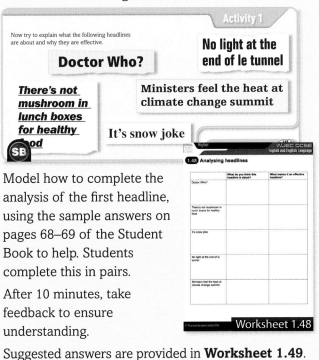

Model how to complete the analysis of the first headline, using the sample answers on pages 68–69 of the Student Book to help. Students complete this in pairs.

After 10 minutes, take feedback to ensure understanding.

Suggested answers are provided in **Worksheet 1.49**.

5 Further work

For homework, students find real examples of headlines or titles that they feel would be worth commenting on in an exam, and also ones that would not be.

Suggested answers

Activity 1, page 69

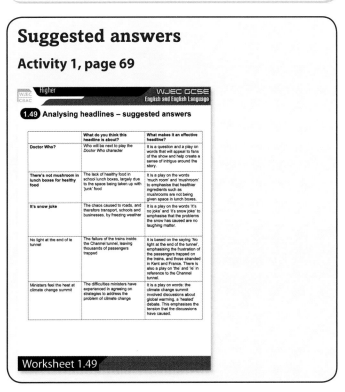

4 Plenary

Read the GradeStudio examiner tips on pages 68–69 of the Student Book.

Distribute copies of **Worksheet 1.50**. Using ActiveTeach, project the worksheet and explain the process of turning the analysis in the table into an exam-style response, and introduce the task.

Working on their own, students complete the task outlined on the worksheet.

After 5 minutes, students swap responses and peer-assess. Ask volunteers to select an effective part of their partner's response to feed back to the class. Encourage them to explain why it is effective.

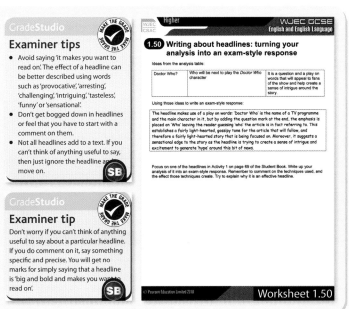

Persuasive pictures and layout
Teaching and learning

Learning Objective
- to understand how pictures and presentation contribute to influencing readers

Required resources
- Student Book, pages 70–71
- Worksheet 1.51: Image selection 1
- Worksheet 1.52: Image selection 2
- Worksheet 1.53: WWF leaflet
- Worksheet 1.54: Activities 1 and 2 – suggested answers

Assessment Objectives
Read and understand texts, selecting material appropriate to purpose, collating from different sources and making comparisons and cross-references as appropriate (English AO2i; English Language AO3i)

1 Starter
Look at the image of the cow on page 70 of the Student Book. How would students describe this image to someone who had not seen it? Look for responses which focus on how the cow is presented.

Distribute/Display **Worksheet 1.51**. Ask students to imagine they are the publisher of a magazine. On the worksheet is a list of articles which will appear in the forthcoming issue. Ask students to write a *brief* for the magazine's picture editor, describing **two** images they want to accompany each article. Point out to students that they should not simply state who or what is in each picture, but how the subject is presented.

- Take feedback to allow students to share their ideas.
- Ask students to identify the 'job' that images do. Look for responses which recognise that images can illustrate and reinforce the message of the text.

2 Paired work
Distribute **Worksheet 1.52**.

Turn to page 70 of the Student Book and read the introduction on persuasive pictures and layout.

> **My learning objective ▼**
> - to understand how pictures and presentation contribute to influencing readers.
>
> **Persuasive pictures and layout**
>
> Visual images convey obvious, and sometimes less obvious, messages. It is usually helpful to think about a picture in relation to the text it accompanies. A picture can illustrate and/or reinforce a message. It can give reality and individuality to someone or something.
>
> A picture may be intended to shock, to attract, or to arouse emotion. Always try to analyse the intention and the effect of pictures in texts. You will get higher marks if you go further than simply describing what is in the picture. Some articles have more than one picture, and you should consider all of them in your response.
>
> When looking at pictures, ask yourself:
> ▶ Why this picture? What is its effect?
> ▶ Is each picture giving the same message?
> ▶ Do the pictures work together to reinforce the message of the text?
> ▶ Do the pictures give different messages? If so, why?
> Remember, a picture will usually link to the headline and the main text.

Students swap their responses (from the Starter activity) on **Worksheet 1.51** with a partner and, using the four bullet points on page 70 of the Student Book, comment on the intended effect of their partner's picture briefs. Students record their responses on **Worksheet 1.52**.

Take feedback to share understanding and reinforce how images can reflect the message of a text.

EAL additional support

Starter:
- **Activate prior knowledge** to elicit sentence starters and phrases which will be useful for 'considering' and commenting on.

Whole-class/paired work
- Add the list of useful questions to interrogate pictures (page 70) to the **word wall** as a reminder that will be useful in future.

- Encourage the students to see any surface meaning/appeal, then ask them to 'think outside the box' to suggest deeper/more original meanings from the picture.

Independent/Activity 1
- Ensure that the pairs are **talk partners**.

Activity 2
Clarify the use and meaning of 'affect' and 'effect' (page 70), which EAL students often confuse. Extend these words with suffixes to illustrate how they are used in sentences.

3 Independent/paired work

Introduce Activity 1 on page 70 of the Student Book. Students complete this activity in pairs. After 5 minutes, take feedback to ensure understanding.

Activity 1

Look at the picture below, then answer the questions that follow.
1 Why this picture? What is its effect?
2 Does the picture reinforce the message of the headline? If so, how?
3 Does the picture give a different message from the headline? If so, how?

Turn to page 71 in the Student Book and introduce Activity 2.

Students complete this task independently.

Activity 2

Working in pairs, identify as many of these logos as you can. For each one, answer the following questions.
1 What does the logo suggest to you?
2 Do you think it is an effective logo? Why/why not?
3 Why did the company or organisation choose this logo?

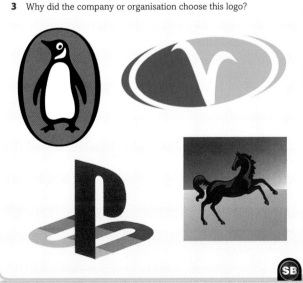

4 Plenary

Recap: ask students to list the eight different persuasive techniques that they should consider when faced with a persuasive text.

Distribute copies of **Worksheet 1.53**. Explain that typical exam questions asking for an analysis of persuasive techniques tend to be phrased 'How does … try to persuade you to…?'

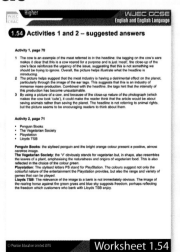

Worksheet 1.53

Ask students to suggest a suitable exam-style question that would go with the leaflet; write it on the board.

Ensuring that they consider a range of persuasive techniques, students list the features they would discuss in an answer to this question. After 5 minutes, students swap lists and peer-assess, checking that all points are valid.

5 Further work

For homework, students revise the eight different persuasive techniques.

Suggested answers

Activities 1 and 2, pages 70–71

Suggested answers for are provided on **Worksheet 1.54**.

Worksheet 1.54

Putting together the persuasive techniques
Teaching and learning and GradeStudio

Required resources
- Student Book, pages 72–76
- Video clip 1.6: *The Apprentice*
- Worksheet 1.55: Putting together the persuasive techniques – Starter
- Worksheet 1.56: Putting together the persuasive technique
- Worksheet 1.57: Analysing your response

Learning Objective
- to understand how writers persuade readers

Assessment Objective
Read and understand texts, selecting material appropriate to purpose, collating from different sources and making comparisons and cross-references as appropriate (English AO2i; English Language AO3i)

1 Starter

Distribute copies of **Worksheet 1.55**. Explain the task, using the instructions on the worksheet. Students are going to watch **Video clip 1.6**, an excerpt from *The Apprentice*. They should listen out for the parts of the pitch that have been identified on the worksheet.

Worksheet 1.55

Video 1.6

Once they viewed the clip, students complete Task 1 on the worksheet in pairs. Take feedback to ensure understanding. Students should then complete Task 2 independently. After 2–3 minutes, hear students' ideas about strengths and weaknesses in the pitch.

Distribute **Worksheet 1.56** and explain the tasks, using the instructions on the worksheet. Give students 2 minutes to complete Task 1, then take feedback to allow them to share some ideas (and help those who didn't have any ideas of their own). Give students 5 minutes to complete task 2.

Worksheet 1.56

Students write their persuasive piece. After 5–7 minutes, partners swap responses and assess how successfully their partner has fulfilled the task, using the checklist of persuasive techniques on the worksheet.

Ask volunteers to read out successful elements from their partner's work, encouraging them to identify the persuasive technique used and to explain why they feel it is successful.

Students suggest what the experience of writing a persuasive text, and peer-assessing the work, can help them to learn about analysing persuasive texts in the exam.

2 Whole-class/paired work

Turn to page 72 of the Student Book and read the letter 'Am I worth £30,000?' and the planning notes for an answer to the question on page 73.

Am I worth £30,000?

Am I worth £30,000? In my career I have been taught skills to save life, prolong life and to know when to walk away when there is no life left. I have taken courses to fight
5 fire from within, above and below. I can cut a car apart in minutes and I can educate your sons and daughters to save their own lives.
No matter what the emergency, I am part of a team that always comes when you call.
10 I run in when all my instincts tell me to run away. I have faced death in cars with petrol pouring over me while the engine was ticking with the heat. I have lain on my back inside a house fire and watched the
15 flames roar across the ceiling above me. I have climbed and I have crawled to save life and I have stood and wept while we buried a fellow firefighter.
I have been the target for yobs throwing
20 stones and punches at me while I do my job. I have been the first to intercept a parent who knows their son is in the car we are cutting up, and I know he is dead. I have served my time, damaged my body and seen
25 th[...] that I hope you never will. I have [...]d 'No, I'm more important than [...]d walked away.

Am I worth £[...] is no. But when [...] your car, or the [...] or your child ne[...] worth every las[...]
Jay Curson
Firefighter, Not[...]

Introduce Activity 1 on page 74. Students complete task 1 in pairs. After 5 minutes, take feedback. Students explain why they have made their choices.

Activity 1

1 In pairs, using the notes on page 73 or your own ideas, write down the main points you think your answer should include.
2 On your own, in no more than 15 minutes, write an answer to the question above.
One of the problems that students have in answering this type of question is finding the right words, often the verbs, to allow them to say precisely what they mean. A range of vocabulary helps you avoid the monotonous repetition of 'the writer says…' You might find some of the following words useful as a way of introducing what you say when you analyse a writer's technique:

- describes
- mentions
- tells
- suggests
- shows
- insists
- compares
- gives details/examples
- emphasises
- uses (examples/facts/statistics/quotations/irony/humour/personal experience)

Using the suggested words listed with task 2, model how to begin an effective answer in response to the question 'How does the letter written to a newspaper by a fireman try to persuade you that his work is worth the £30,000 a year he is paid?', e.g. *The writer **uses** a rhetorical question as both his headline and his very first sentence, which **emphasises** how much he wants the readers to… . In the second sentence the writer **describes** different skills he has been taught…* or *he **mentions** the fact that one of his skills is to 'know when to walk away when there is no life left', etc.*

EAL additional support

Starter

- **Active listening:** the teacher or fluent class readers should read the text aloud using clear expression, pauses, gestures and facial expression to facilitate understanding of the repressed emotion of the <u>firefighter</u>.
- **Talk partners**: pair an EAL student with a fluent English student to discuss the different aspects of the text. The list on page 73 of the Student Book: content, language, tone, etc. are very helpful and could be put on a **word wall** or **washing line** as reminders for the future.
- **Text highlight** examples of the different techniques in the texts.

Am I worth £30,000?

- Clarify socio-cultural, idiomatic, technical, language and words with multiple meanings, e.g. 'fire within', 'instincts', 'yobs', 'intercept', '£30K', 'drunk', 'penny'…as appropriate.

Fastest lady on two wheels

- Remind students of the work in Lesson 9.
- Clarify socio-cultural, idiomatic, technical, language and words with multiple meanings, e.g. 'gargantuan', 'pillion seat', 'revs up', 'opens the throttle', 'higher than a kite', 'to black out' as necessary.
- Use the 'Putting into practice' and 'In the future' sections on page 79 as short **dictogloss** activities – as an aide memoire.

3 Independent work

Give students 12–15 minutes to finish producing a full answer to task 2 of Activity 1.

Distribute copies of **Worksheet 1.57**. Students follow the instructions to analyse the response they have just written. Once they have annotated their work, students mark and grade their own work, using the Peer/Self-assessment qustions on page 75 of the Student Book.

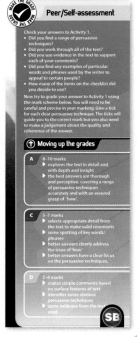

4 Plenary

Read 'The Fastest Lady on Two Wheels' on page 76 of the Student Book. In pairs, students list points that could be included in an answer to the question 'How does Petronella Wyatt get across to you what it is like to ride the TT course?'

After 5 minutes, take feedback, encouraging students to explain why their chosen point would be effective in an answer.

Suggested answers

Activity 1, Task 1, page 74

- Details all the skills and experience he has
- tells the reader how dangerous the job is – and how reliable and courageous fire officers are
- contrasts money with the value of life
- persuasive techniques: rhetorical questions, triplets, repetition, emotional appeal to reader.

Putting together the persuasive techniques
GradeStudio and Assessment

Learning Objectives
- to practise analysing persuasive writing
- to develop a secure technique for answering this type of question

Required resources
- Student Book, pages 76–81
- Worksheet 1.58: Sample responses
- Worksheet 1.59: A/A* mark scheme

Assessment Objectives
Read and understand texts, selecting material appropriate to purpose, collating from different sources and making comparisons and cross-references as appropriate (English AO2i; English Language AO3i)

1 Starter

Distribute copies of **Worksheet 1.58**, which contains the two sample responses from pages 77–78 of the Student Book and read the instructions at the top of the page. Students complete the analysis of the responses in pairs. After 10 minutes, they can use pages 77–78 of the Student Book to check their analysis.

2 Whole-class/ paired work

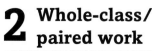

Turn to page 79 of the Student Book and read 'Persuasive techniques: how to go up the grades'.

Display **Worksheet 1.59** to show the A/A* criteria for this sort of question, and re-establish what is required to achieve top marks.

Using ActiveTeach, display Student 2's response on page 78 of the Student Book. Starting with the parts of the response that received less positive comments from the examiner, model how to make changes to improve the answer. In pairs, students continue to improve this response, aiming to make it an A* answer. After 5 minutes, take one piece of feedback from each pair, using students' ideas to keep making changes to the displayed response.

Once all pairs have given feedback and the response has been altered all the way through, distribute the A/A* mark schemes and ask students to assess whether the new response would deserve a higher grade.

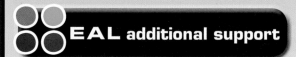
EAL additional support

Starter

Students should be reminded that, when exploring viewpoint/attitude, thoughts, feelings, a single word, short phrases or prefixes are all appropriate ways of informing the reader which can be used as evidence.

The teacher should emphasise such words and phrases whilst completing the first two examples in worksheet 1.58, and model orally how to quote them to answer an exam question.

Activity 2
- The text describes an event which is probably outside EAL learners' knowledge and experience, not only the 'Isle of Man' and 'TT course' but also 'ravine', 'pillion', 'scooters' and 'leathers' so it would be beneficial to
- share prior knowledge
- discuss the picture
- perhaps liken it to a rollercoaster ride to explain feelings
- There should be awareness that socio-cultural idiomatic language such as 'mouth of death', 'jaws of Hell', 'hairpin bend' and 'weedy' should also be explored and explained as evidence of thoughts, feelings and attitude.
- Pair work should mix a 'good' language role model with an EAL learner.

3 Interactive GradeStudio

Open the interactive GradeStudio activity using ActiveTeach.

The objective of this activity is for students to understand the mark scheme.

Use this activity at the front of the class to assess sample answers at every grade, using the highlight tool and questions to assess the strengths and weaknesses of the answers. Students put themselves in the position of the examiner and reward the sample answers a grade.

4 Independent work

Introduce Activity 1 on pages 80–81. Independently, students read the article and write a response to the question. After 15 minutes, they check their answers using the mark scheme on page 81.

5 Plenary

Students swap responses with a partner. Using the criteria on page 81, peers assess each other's work. Students feed back their comments and targets to each other.

Turning back to page 79, pairs discuss the points identified in the 'Putting it into practice' box.

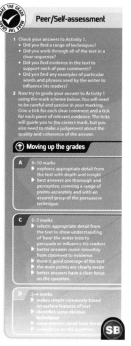

6 Further work

For homework, students develop the A/A* mark scheme into a more detailed checklist that would help them achieve high grades in future analyses of persuasive techniques.

Suggested answers

Activity 1, page 80

Note: 'How' is partly a matter of content/presentation and partly a matter of language/structure. Look for a clear sense of 'how' as opposed to simply 'what'. The best answers take the 'extra step' to analyse the detail rather than spotting it.

Some key points:
- He calls the amateur event 'Mad Sunday' (it is a form of insanity).
- The amateurs are described as 'crazy'.
- The riders are called 'wildcats' who risk their lives.
- He compares the race fairground switchbacks and the 'wall of death'.
- He refers to 'wild enthusiasm' and 'hurling' themselves around the course (deliberate risking of life and limb).

- He uses figures to show the alarming speeds ('even 150mph').
- He calls the event on Sunday 'chaos'.
- The authorities try to reduce the numbers but the riders are 'determined'.
- He uses the example of Mark Farmer to show it is a case of life and death.
- The crash was 'horrific'.
- He uses facts and figures about casualties – ten deaths last year (including spectators), six crashes this year 'in the first practice on Monday', 20 serious injuries each year).
- Quotes local journalist suggesting 170 deaths over the years.
- Quotes Steve Hislop to show just how dangerous and mad it is.

Comparing and contrasting texts
Teaching and learning and GradeStudio

Required resources
- Student Book, pages 76, 80–87
- Video clip 1.7: *Midlands Today* Treasure Hoard
- Video clip 1.8: National News Hoard story
- Worksheet 1.60: Comparing and contrasting texts
- Worksheet 1.61: Comparing and contrasting views on the smoking ban
- Worksheet 1.62: Comparing and contrasting views on the smoking ban – suggested answers

Learning Objectives
- to learn how to compare and contrast two texts
- to understand how to approach this type of question

Assessment Objectives
Read and understand texts, selecting material appropriate to purpose, collating from different sources and making comparisons and cross-references as appropriate (English AO2i; English Language AO3i)

1 Starter

Distribute copies of **Worksheet 1.60** and read the instructions at the top of the page.

Using ActiveTeach, play **Video clips 1.7** and **1.8**. Students watch carefully to pick out the relevant points of comparison and how these are presented in each clip.

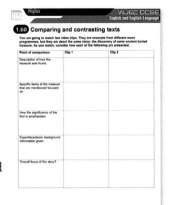
Worksheet 1.60

Video 1.7

Video 1.8

Play both video clips twice. Once students have viewed the clips, allow them 2 minutes to share and consolidate their responses with a partner. Take feedback to ensure understanding.

2 Whole-class/paired work

'Compare and contrast' questions

These questions ask you to look for specific similarities and differences in the two texts. Your personal views and opinions are not required. You will waste time and get no marks if you ignore the question and simply give your views about the texts or the issues they discuss.

These questions look like this:

1 These two texts give very different impressions. In what ways are they different?

2 Compare and contrast what these two texts tell you about…

3 These two texts are about… Compare and contrast them using the following headings…

In this type of question you will often be given a list of bullet points to follow, and you should use them to structure your answer. If you are told to organise your answer into paragraphs using the bullet points as headings, then you should do exactly that. Remember that the examiner is trying to help you and you should take whatever help is offered.

Comparing and contrasting is a skill that requires clarity of thought and organisation. The candidates who handle this type of question well are those who can stand back and see the broad picture. The supporting detail from the text can then be used purposefully. Try to avoid including personal views and opinions which can lead to long but unfocused answers.

Sometimes it is possible to see that both texts are making the and it is economical when you can claim that 'both texts' say don't force the similarities. There will probably be differences

Turn to page 82 of the Student Book and read the introduction to 'Comparing and contrasting texts'.

Introduce Activity 1 on pages 84–85. Read both texts. Pairs spend 3 minutes considering similarities between the two texts. Take feedback. Then distribute copies of **Worksheet 1.61**, which contains a planning table for task 2 of Activity 1. Using the instructions on the worksheet, explain the task. Students work in pairs to complete their tables.

EAL additional support

Introduction: whole-class/pair work
- **Active listening:** read around the class all the advice on page 82, including the examiner tip.
- Clarify any difficult words.
- **Talk partners:** spend time to establish firmly the meaning of 'compare and contrast' – often difficult concepts for the EAL students.

Activity 1
- **Active listening:** carefully read both texts about the smoking ban. Clarify any difficulties with socio-cultural, idiomatic, technical, language and

words with multiple meanings, e.g. 'flaws', 'pub', 'unwind', 'outcasts'…(Extract 1) and 'overwhelming', 'addictiveness', 'infringe', 'second-hand smoking', 'annually', 'melodramatic', 'over-the-top'…(Extract 2).
- Use a **mind map** to analyse the two texts, noting similarities and differences or highlight the text.
- Select words from the **word wall** and use **sentence starters/writing frames** to revise work on the language of contrasting and comparing, e.g. 'comparatives', 'but', 'however', 'whereas'.

GradeStudio
Carefully **analyse** the A and A* texts, **highlighting** particularly effective details in the A* answer which make it the better than the A answer.

3 Independent work

After 10 minutes, students work on their own to produce a response to the question 'Compare and contrast the views of these two writers on the subject of the ban on smoking in public places'.

Students now turn to pages 76 and 80–81 of the Student Book and read the two texts about the TT races on the Isle of Man, and the student answers on pages 86–87.

Students compare their response to Activity 1, task 2 on page 85 to these answers, reflecting on areas of strength and considering the target areas they should work on.

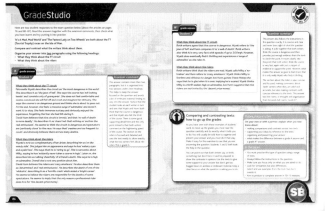

4 Interactive GradeStudio

Open the interactive GradeStudio activity using ActiveTeach.

The objective of this activity is to understand what skills are required at different grades, and that there are different ways to achieve the same grade. This activity gives a range of sample answers for each grade.

At the front of the class analyse and compare the answers to the same grade, and compare the answer at different grades.

Discuss the examiner comments with the class so that students can understand what skills are required at each grade and see that there are different ways to achieve the same grade.

Students will become familiar with the criteria specific to each grade. Students will also be shown the best way to arrive at that grade. In addition, by comparing answers to the same question the students can see how questions are commonly misinterpreted and marks are lost.

5 Plenary

Using the understanding they have gained, students now work in pairs to write a mark scheme for A* responses to 'Compare and contrast' questions. Take feedback and consolidate responses to create a class checklist.

Pairs discuss the 'Putting it into practice' bullet points on page 87 of the Student Book.

Putting it into practice

On your own or with a partner, explain what you now know about:
- making comparisons and contrasts across two texts
- supporting your ideas by reference to the texts
- organising and presenting your answer
- what makes the difference between a grade A answer and a grade A* answer.

Suggested answers

Activity 1, task 1, pages 84–85

Suggested answers are provided on **Worksheet 1.62.**

Worksheet 1.62

Using information from two texts
Teaching and learning and GradeStudio

Learning Objectives
- to use information from two texts
- to learn how to approach this type of question

Required resources
- Student Book, pages 76, 80–81, 88–95
- Worksheet 1.63: Using information from two texts
- Worksheet 1.64: Sample responses

Assessment Objectives
Read and understand texts, selecting material appropriate to purpose, collating from different sources and making comparisons and cross-references as appropriate (English AO2i; English Language AO3i)

1 Starter

Distribute copies of **Worksheet 1.63** and turn back to the two extracts about the TT races on pages 76 and 80–81 of the Student Book. Students complete the tasks on their worksheets in pairs.

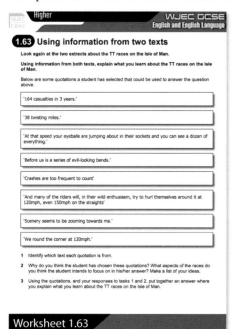

Allow 3 minutes for the first two tasks and take feedback after each to ensure understanding.

Allow 5–7 minutes for task 3, then hear some of the students' responses and encourage them to explain the choices they made.

Explain to students that the activities on their worksheets have provided them with the essential steps needed to approach this type of question. Students identify what these steps are.

2 Whole-class/paired work

Use page 88 of the Student Book to reinforce explanation of how to approach 'Using information from two texts' questions.

Introduce Activity 1 on page 89, then read the two texts on pages 90–91.

In pairs, with one student taking responsibility for each text, students list the relevant information in the texts. Pairs compare information and select the points that will create the most coherent answer. After 10 minutes, take feedback and list points on the board. Reinforce the importance of identifying relevant information from both texts, and that it makes sense to identify where the information has come from.

Starter
- **Active listening:** careful reading of the two texts will provide an opportunity to **revise** any difficulties with vocabulary.

Whole-class/paired work
- Read the explanation and examiner tip on page 88 aloud around the class.
- **Talk partners:** pair the students to discuss the difference between the compare/contrast tasks of the last lesson and the collecting information from the two texts task of this lesson.

Activity 1
- Before reading the question, remind students of **T**ext **A**udience **P**urpose (TAP), then emphasise the key words 'make a <u>list</u>' (T) ...<u>parents</u> (A) <u>tips</u>...on how to cope...'
- **Envoys** or **text highlighting** could be used as alternative strategies: create paired groups to make notes about one text, then send an envoy to the other group, which then identifies points similar to those in the text they analysed. Then the groups come together to compare notes.
- Use **message abundancy** to clarify idiomatic language, e.g. 'showered with gifts', 'going into meltdown'.

3 Independent work
Turn to pages 92–93 of the Student Book and introduce the next task. Students read both extracts and list the ideas they feel are relevant for the question.

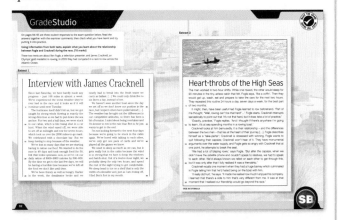

After 10 minutes, distribute copies of **Worksheet 1.64**. Students rank the student responses on the worksheet, then identify any strengths and weaknesses they can see in each answer and write these ideas in the 'Your comments' column.

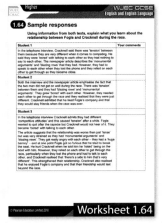

4 Plenary
Take feedback, encouraging full explanation of the strengths and weaknesses that students have identified. Using pages 94–95 of the Student Book, students compare their comments to the examiner's.

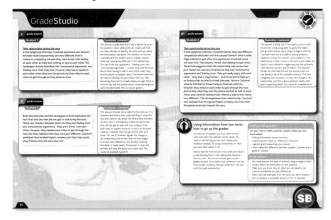

In pairs, students discuss the 'Putting it into practice' bullet points on page 95 of the Student Book. Take feedback and establish a class checklist of key things to remember when faced with this sort of question.

5 Further work
For homework, students find two texts that are linked, then write three different exam-style questions to demonstrate their understanding of the comparison and evaluation of texts aspect of the exam.

Suggested answers

Activity 1, page 89
Extract 1
- 'Keep a constant supply of coke, crisps and sweets in the house'
- 'Don't offer them a healthy meal' to avoid tantrums
- 'Never enter their room without knocking'
- 'Give them something to do! Buy them games, DVDs, CDs, magazines'

- Don't ask about their social life
- Don't embarrass them in front of their friends
- Don't ask about school, homework or revision.

Extract 2
- 'Hide' during the teenage years
- 'Exit the room' for mood swings
- Don't go into their rooms, or 'only enter when they are out'.

Writing an informal letter

Learning Objectives

- to learn about the layout and organisation of an informal letter
- to learn how style, tone and content work together to achieve effect

Required resources

- Student Book, pages 100–107
- Worksheet 2.1: Formal and informal language
- Worksheet 2.2: Formal and informal language – spectrum
- Worksheet 2.3: Greetings – starter display
- Worksheet 2.4: layout of an informal letter
- Worksheet 2.5: Letter layout annotations
- Worksheet 2.6: Peer/Self-assessment

Assessment Objectives

Write clearly, effectively and imaginatively, using and adapting forms and selecting vocabulary appropriate to task and purpose in ways which engage the reader (English AO3i; English Language AO4i)

1 Starter

Distribute copies of **Worksheet 2.1** and use the instructions on the worksheet to explain the task. Students work on task 1 in pairs. Take feedback once students have created their formal to informal spectrum.

Display **Worksheet 2.2**.

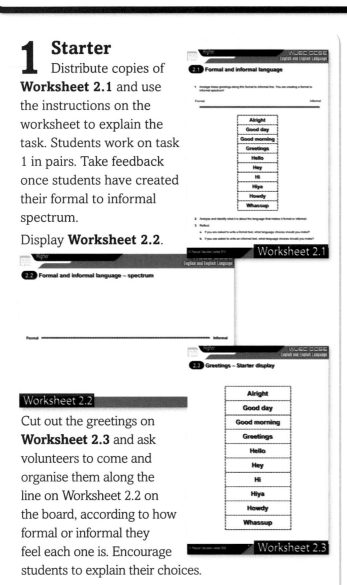

Cut out the greetings on **Worksheet 2.3** and ask volunteers to come and organise them along the line on Worksheet 2.2 on the board, according to how formal or informal they feel each one is. Encourage students to explain their choices.

Model how to analyse language by focusing on the greetings at the ends of the spectrum. Highlight significant features such as altered spellings or merged words to create different styles of greetings.

Pairs complete tasks 2 and 3 on **Worksheet 2.1**. Explain that they will be drawing on this understanding to help them with their work on formal and informal letters.

2 Whole-class/paired work

Display page 100 of the Student Book and introduce the Learning Objectives.

Complete Activity 1, task 1 by taking suggestions from the class and creating a list on the board.

Give pairs 3 minutes to complete Activity 1, task 2. Take feedback from pairs to establish the most important features of informal letters.

Using ActiveTeach, display **Worksheet 2.4**, which contains the model letter from page 101 of the Student Book. Distribute copies of **Worksheet 2.5** to students. Pairs decide where each comment belongs, then stick the comments to the board accordingly.

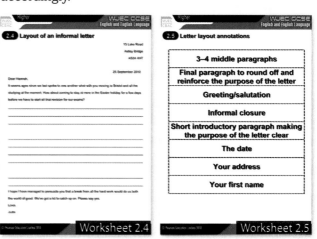

Consolidate the learning so far by asking students to reiterate when they might write an informal letter, what its key features are and what its layout should be.

3 Independent work

Students complete Activity 2, task 1 on page 101 of the Student Book. Once they have written their letter, they should compare their response to the three featured in GradeStudio as instructed in Activity 2, task 2.

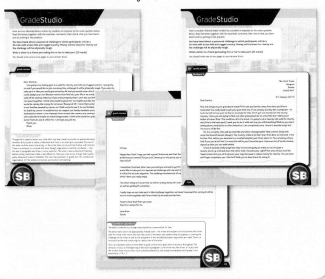

4 Plenary

Turn to the letter on page 106 of the Student Book. Read the letter with the class and ask students to comment on strengths and weaknesses.

In pairs, students complete Activity 3. After 5 minutes, students swap their work with another pair and peer-assess the letter.

Ask: What are the key things to remember about completing this task successfully? (Use the appropriate layout, keep language choices suitably informal, make use of words and phrases that suggest a relationship between you and the person you are writing to, etc.)

5 Further work

For homework, ask students to complete Activity 4's letter-writing task on page 107 of the Student Book. Distribute copies of **Worksheet 2.6** for students to use to assess their work, once they have written their letters.

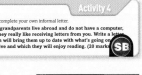

Suggested answers

Activity 3, page 106

- There is no date or informal closure.
- The student doesn't start addressing the question properly until the second paragraph, and even then the ideas are underdeveloped/thin in terms of present suggestions and reasons for those suggestions.
- Though they are underdeveloped, the paragraphs help to organise the different ideas in the response.
- The opening and closing are relatively effective because they help create a sense of relationship between grandparents and grandchild. However, the content isn't completely believable – the 'so I don't have to write so much' doesn't fit with the opening 'I can't believe that I'm using a pen', and the 'don't forget me!' doesn't ring true.
- In places the tone is appropriate, but there are lapses: 'me and the family are fine' suddenly makes Toby sound less like a grandson and more like an adult son who is a parent himself.
- Accuracy:
  - there are three spelling mistakes: 'writing', 'momment', and 'give' where 'given' was meant.
  - there are many missing full stops: 'The last time I saw you was at Sue and Dave's wedding _ me and the family are fine _ Andrew has just started junior school…'
  - apostrophes are accurate.
  - there is some misuse of capital letters: 'Andrew has Just started…' and 'get them a Nintendo DS game each Because…'

Writing a formal letter

Learning Objectives

- to learn about approaches to writing formal letters
- to understand the key differences between formal and informal letters

Required resources

- Student Book, pages 108–115
- Video clip 2.1: Planet Earth
- Worksheet 2.7: Planning the content
- Worksheet 2.8: Sample A* letter
- Worksheet 2.8a: Activity 3 – Suggested answers
- Worksheet 2.9: Peer/Self-assessment

Assessment Objectives

Write clearly, effectively and imaginatively, using and adapting forms and selecting vocabulary appropriate to task and purpose in ways which engage the reader (English AO3i; English Language AO4i)

1 Starter

For Activity 1, task 1, on page 108 of the Student Book pairs discuss occasions when they might need to write a formal letter. After 1 minute, take some suggestions.

> **Activity 1**
> 1 Make a list of occasions when you might need to write a formal letter.
> SB

Using ActiveTeach, watch **Video clip 2.1**. As students watch, they should note down examples of language used which indicate the level of formality in this text. Ask students to use

Video 2.1

some of the language they have identified, and some of the points made in the video, to write the opening two or three sentences of a formal letter to their MP in which they highlight the issue raised in the video.

Ask students to re-use the same content to write an informal letter to a friend, drawing their attention to the same issue.

Take feedback, highlighting how students have changed their language choice according to audience.

Turn to page 108 of the Student Book to explore the ways, other than language choice, in which formal and informal letters differ.

Audience	In this type of letter you will be writing to a person you may not know personally or who you know in a more formal way. It might be a potential employer, a council official, a newspaper editor or a headteacher. This will clearly make a difference to the way in which you write the letter. The language and tone will be quite different from the chatty style of the letters we have looked at so far. Most letters of this type take a fairly serious approach.
Purpose	This could be to apply for a job, to give your view on an issue of concern to you, to complain etc. Whatever its purpose, it is important that your letter uses an appropriate tone. If you are writing a job application, you will want to impress; if you are writing on an issue of concern to you, you may, of course, express those views strongly and forcefully, but you should always be polite.
Format	This is different from the format of an informal letter. Again, you will include your address and the date, but this time you will also include the address of the recipient (the person you are writing to). (In the exam you may be given the address, but if not, you should make one up). The salutation will, in this case, be more formal, e.g. 'Dear Mr Asson' or 'Dear Sir/Madam' if you do not know the name of the person. The closure if you do not know the person's name will be 'Yours faithfully'. If you started the letter 'Dear Mrs Baker', then the letter should end 'Yours sincerely'.
Content	The question will tell you what the content should be, but whatever the topic, you must plan your letter. Think about your opening paragraph and then about the central points and how you intend to express them. Arguing or putting across your points logically is important and strengthens your case. Put yourself in the position of the recipient. The organisation will be similar to that suggested for the informal letter: • a fairly brief opening paragraph in which you outline/introduce your reason for writing • three or four central paragraphs in which you put your case • a final paragraph that rounds off the letter.

2 Whole-class/paired work

Distribute copies of **Worksheet 2.7** and give students 1 minute to complete task 1. Use the instructions on the worksheet to explain task 2.

In pairs, students complete the table on the worksheet with their ideas about the smoking ban. After 5–7 minutes, take feedback to allow students to share ideas. They should make a note of any ideas they hear that they agree with.

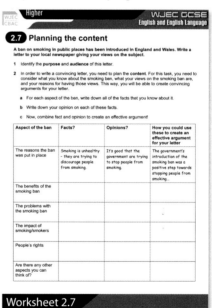

Worksheet 2.7

Working in pairs, students then complete the planning task outlined in Activity 2, task 1, on page 109 of the Student Book.

> **Activity 2**
> 1 A ban on smoking in public places has been introduced in England and Wales, and you are going to write a letter to your local newspaper giving your views on the subject.
>
> With a partner:
> • show how you would set out the letter
> • plan your opening paragraph
> • next, think about your honestly held views on the subject of smoking in public places and include two or three substantial points you can make for or against. These will be dealt with in your central paragraphs, i.e. one for each paragraph
> • plan your concluding paragraph which will round off the letter.
> SB

Starter
- **L1 discussion**: pairs of EAL students who share L1 could discuss when they would need to write formally and what conventions are important in their L1.

Activity 1
- **Talk partners**: pair EAL students with fluent English speakers to revise audience, purpose, format, content terms used in the previous lesson and extend to formal letters using the table and layout on pages 108–109.

- **Word wall**: make cards for purpose, audience, format and content for a semi-permanent display and ready reference through all the lessons on writing.

Whole-class work/paired work
- Use a **mind map** or other **key visual/graphic organiser** to plan the content of the letter and **sequence** into a logical order.
- **ICT-based tools**: repeat the activity from the previous lesson but use the components of a formal letter.

As a **scaffold**, use one the A* letters as a **dictogloss**. Then one group could reproduce it as a letter of complaint whilst the other writes a letter to support the issue.

3 Independent work

Students complete Activity 2, task 2 independently. Once they have written their letter, they should compare their work with the three responses provided in GradeStudio, as instructed in Activity 2, task 3.

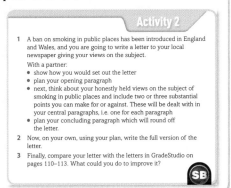

Activity 2

1. A ban on smoking in public places has been introduced in England and Wales, and you are going to write a letter to your local newspaper giving your views on the subject.
   With a partner:
   - show how you would set out the letter
   - plan your opening paragraph
   - next, think about your honestly held views on the subject of smoking in public places and include two or three substantial points you can make for or against. These will be dealt with in your central paragraphs, i.e. one for each paragraph
   - plan your concluding paragraph which will round off the letter.
2. Now, on your own, using your plan, write the full version of the letter.
3. Finally, compare your letter with the letters in GradeStudio on pages 110–113. What could you do to improve it? **SB**

4 Interactive GradeStudio

Open the interactive GradeStudio activity using ActiveTeach.

The objective of this activity is to help students self-assess their work against the mark scheme and to identify how to achieve higher marks.

This activity is an opportunity for students to assess their own work with the examiner's help. It is suited to students working independently at a computer rather than the whole class. Students can time themselves typing an answer to the set question or they can paste in an answer they have already written to the question.

When they have finished writing, they choose the grade they think they have achieved from the mark scheme. The examiner helps them to check whether they have reached this grade with a series of questions.

Finally, the student can rework their answer with the feedback or print it out for the teacher to check. The answer they have written can also be saved.

5 Plenary

Using ActiveTeach, display **Worksheet 2.8**, which contains the A* letter from page 114 of the Student Book. Distribute copies to students. Read the letter with the class and ask students to comment on its strengths and weaknesses.

Worksheet 2.8

Turn to page 114 of the Student Book and introduce Activity 3.

Activity 3

This letter was awarded an A* grade in the examination (12/13 for content and organisation and 7/7 for sentence structure, punctuation and spelling). Note that the real version of the letter contained the writer's and recipient's address and the date.
Use the questions below to explain why this was given such a high mark.
- How has the letter been organised?
- How effective are the introduction and conclusion?
- What are the features of the central paragraphs? How persuasive and lively are they?
- How accurate is the writing? Look at the spelling of familiar and less familiar words. For example, 'business' is often misspelt and 'adrenaline' isn't easy.
- How effective is the use of apostrophes, question marks and commas?
- Look also at the way in which sentences have been constructed. Is there variety in sentence length and type?
- If you were a newspaper editor, would you print this letter? Explain why. **SB**

In pairs, students annotate the letter with their answers to the bullet points. After 5 minutes, students feed back their findings. Use their comments to annotate the letter on the board.

Establish a class checklist of the key differences between formal and informal letters.

6 Further work

For homework, students complete the letter-writing task in Activity 4, page 115 of the Student Book. Distribute copies of **Worksheet 2.9**, for students to use to assess their work, once they have written their letters.

Activity 4

Now complete your own formal letter using the following question set in the exam.
A **TV magazine** has invited readers to give their views on the standard of programmes on television. The magazine is offering a prize for the best response. Write your letter. (20 marks) **SB**

Worksheet 2.9

Suggested answers

Activity 3, page 114
Suggested answers are provided on **Worksheet 2.8a**

Worksheet 2.8a

Writing a report
Teaching and learning and GradeStudio

Learning Objectives
- to understand the nature of a report
- to learn how to plan, organise and complete such a report

Required resources
- Student Book, pages 116–119
- Worksheet 2.10: A teacher's report
- Worksheet 2.11: Sample student report

Assessment Objectives
Write clearly, effectively and imaginatively, using and adapting forms and selecting vocabulary appropriate to task and purpose in ways which engage the reader (English AO3i; English Language AO4i)

1 Starter

Give students 2 minutes to discuss in pairs what they understand a 'report' to be. They should think about different kinds of reports they may have read or written. Take feedback to allow students to share ideas.

Students complete Activity 1 on page 116 and create a checklist that includes the key features of a report.

Distribute copies of **Worksheet 2.10**, which gets students looking at the key features of a report. Using the instructions on the worksheet, explain the tasks. Students complete tasks 1 and 2 in pairs.

Now display the worksheet using ActiveTeach. After 5–7 minutes, take feedback from students and use their ideas to annotate the reports on the whiteboard. With the class, establish what this shows about purpose, format, audience and tone in reports.

Students use this understanding to complete task 4. After 3–5 minutes, ask volunteers to read out their reports. Students assess how successfully their partner has addressed purpose, format, audience and tone.

Activity 1

What kinds of reports have you read or written? You have all received school reports. Read through the notes below and share what you know about the different audiences and purposes for reports. Create a checklist that could be used by someone starting to write a report. Try to include all of the key features of a report in your checklist.

Purpose	The purpose of a report is to inform, advise or persuade a person or a group of people. It is normally written after something has been researched/investigated/thought about, for example the provision of public transport in an area. It gives up-to-date information to those who need it and can act upon it.
Format	There will be a clear and uncomplicated format so that the points raised are presented clearly to the reader(s). There will be a main heading and probably sub-headings, since the report is likely to consider different aspects of the subject. The clear separation of these points will help the reader(s) and will give shape and organisation to the work.
Audience	Most reports are written in a formal manner, though to a certain extent this can depend on who they are for. This might be your local council, your headteacher or your school council. The stated audience will, of course, help you to decide how the report is to be written. It will be more formal for the local council than for your fellow students, but even in this case there will be some formality.
Tone	This will be respectful, but that does not mean that you cannot put your views strongly. Making your points so that there can be no misunderstanding is not the same as being rude. Your points should be based on evidence and should be clearly made.

Worksheet 2.10

2 Whole-class/paired work

Turn to page 116 of the Student Book to reinforce the ideas generated in the Starter.

Using ActiveTeach, display the sample student report on page 117, and distribute copies of **Worksheet 2.11**.

Worksheet 2.11

Read the report. Ask the class to work backwards: What must this student's plan have looked like? Give students 3 minutes to work in pairs on creating a plan. Take feedback. Use students' ideas to reinforce the importance of a logical plan for this task.

Explain that students are going to highlight the text where they can see awareness of purpose, format, audience and tone. Model how to do this, then allow pairs 5 minutes to work on this task.

Students identify any similarities or differences they have noticed between this report and the teacher's report on **Worksheet 2.10**.

3 Independent work

Introduce Activity 2 on page 117 of the Student Book. Students plan their reports by following the advice in the Student Book, then write their reports independently.

4 Interactive GradeStudio

Open the interactive GradeStudio activity using ActiveTeach.

The objective of this activity is to understand what skills are required at different grades, and that there are different ways to achieve the same grade. This activity gives a range of sample answers for each grade.

At the front of the class analyse and compare the answers to the same grade, and compare the answer at different grades.

Discuss the examiner comments with the class so that students can understand what skills are required at each grade and see that there are different ways to achieve the same grade.

Students will become familiar with the criteria specific to each grade. Students will also be shown the best way to arrive at that grade. In addition, by comparing answers to the same question the students can see how questions are commonly misinterpreted and marks are lost.

5 Plenary

Students swap reports with a partner and peer-assess their work, using the report on pages 118–19 of the Student Book. Students feed back their comments to each other, then reflect on their performance and decide on a target area to focus on in the next lesson.

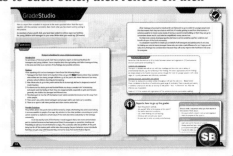

Writing a report
Exam practice and assessment

Learning Objectives
- to practise using key features of a report
- to develop a secure approach to writing a report

Required resources
- Student Book, pages 120–121
- Worksheet 2.12: Improving a C-grade report
- Worksheet 2.13: Planning the report
- Worksheet 2.14: Sample responses

Assessment Objectives
Write clearly, effectively and imaginatively, using and adapting forms and selecting vocabulary appropriate to task and purpose in ways which engage the reader (English AO3i; English Language AO4i)

1 Starter
Distribute copies of **Worksheet 2.12**, which contains the C-grade response from page 120 of the Student Book. Use the instructions on the worksheet to explain the tasks. Students complete the tasks in pairs.

Using ActiveTeach, display the C-grade response on page 120 of the Student Book. After 10 minutes, take feedback from students and use their ideas to annotate the report. Students summarise what they can learn from this.

2 Whole-class/paired work
Turn to Activity 2 on page 121 of the Student Book. Distribute copies of **Worksheet 2.13**. Students complete task 1 on the worksheet in pairs. Once students have ideas for their report, they should write a plan for it.

Activity 2

Now complete your own report in response to the exam question below.

Write a report for your headteacher/principal about the ways in which your school/college prepares you for the world outside school/college. You may consider both the positive and the negative aspects. Remember the importance of format, audience and purpose. (20 marks)

Higher   WJEC GCSE
                                    English and English Language

2.13 Planning the report

Write a report for your headteacher/principal about the ways in which your school/college prepares you for the world outside school/college. You may consider both the positive and the negative aspects. Remember the importance of format, audience and purpose.

Before you write your report, it is useful to generate some ideas. You can then use these ideas to write an effective plan for your answer.

1 Complete the table below.

For the world outside school or college, how will you need to be prepared?	What things your school or college do to prepare you? How successful are these things?	What else could your school or college do? How could current systems be improved?

2 Use the ideas you have generated to write a plan for your report. Remember to think carefully about your headings, and about making your points in a convincing fashion.

Worksheet 2.13

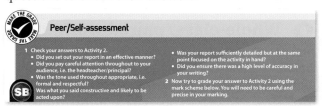

EAL additional support

Starter
- **Active listening** read around the class the notes on purpose, format, audience and tone from the table. Clarify any difficult words.
- **L1 discussion**: pairs of EAL students who share L1 could discuss when they would need to write reports and what conventions are important in their L1.
- Or use **talk partners**: pair EAL student with a fluent English speaker to discuss the types of reports they know together.

- **Word Wall**: make cards for purpose, audience, format and content for a semi-permanent display and ready reference through all the lessons on writing.
- **Active listening**: The teacher should read the student's report on page 120 using expression, pauses, gestures and facial expression to aid understanding and revise tone.
- **select/highlight** phrases which illustrate the points – this will be a scaffold for future work.
- Use **talk partners** to work through the improving a C grade report.

Activity 3
Students could use **mind map** or other **key visual/graphic organiser** to plan the content of their report.

3 Independent work

Students write their reports for Activity 2 independently, then use the Peer/Self-assessment questions to check their answers.

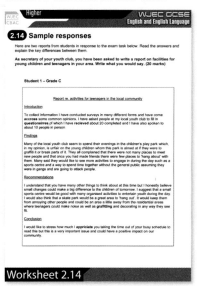

Peer/Self-assessment

1 Check your answers to Activity 2.
- Did you set out your report in an effective manner?
- Did you pay careful attention throughout to your audience, i.e. the headteacher/principal?
- Was the tone used throughout appropriate, i.e. formal and respectful?
- Was what you said constructive and likely to be acted upon?
- Was your report sufficiently detailed but at the same point focused on the activity in hand?
- Did you ensure there was a high level of accuracy in your writing?

2 Now try to grade your answer to Activity 2 using the mark scheme below. You will need to be careful and precise in your marking.

5 Further work

For homework, students create a student revision guide page, giving advice on effective report-writing.

4 Plenary

Students swap their reports with a partner and use the mark scheme on page 121 of the Student Book to grade their peer's response. They should annotate the response where they can see aspects of the mark scheme being fulfilled. They should also make any suggestions for improvement.

Distribute copies of **Worksheet 2.14**, which contains two sample responses. Students should try to explain the key differences between the two reports, and what those differences show about how to achieve success in this task.

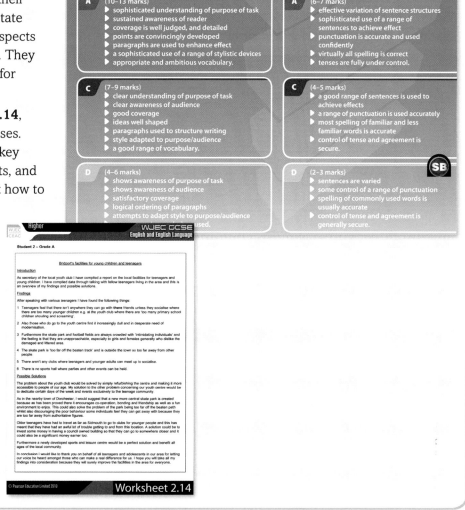

Moving up the grades

Content and organisation (13 marks)	Sentence structure, punctuation and spelling (7 marks)
A (10–13 marks) ▸ sophisticated understanding of purpose of task ▸ sustained awareness of reader ▸ coverage is well judged, and detailed ▸ points are convincingly developed ▸ paragraphs are used to enhance effect ▸ a sophisticated use of a range of stylistic devices ▸ appropriate and ambitious vocabulary.	**A** (6–7 marks) ▸ effective variation of sentence structures ▸ sophisticated use of a range of sentences to achieve effect ▸ punctuation is accurate and used confidently ▸ virtually all spelling is correct ▸ tenses are fully under control.
C (7–9 marks) ▸ clear understanding of purpose of task ▸ clear awareness of audience ▸ good coverage ▸ ideas well shaped ▸ paragraphs used to structure writing ▸ style adapted to purpose/audience ▸ a good range of vocabulary.	**C** (4–5 marks) ▸ a good range of sentences is used to achieve effects ▸ a range of punctuation is used accurately ▸ most spelling of familiar and less familiar words is accurate ▸ control of tense and agreement is secure.
D (4–6 marks) ▸ shows awareness of purpose of task ▸ shows awareness of audience ▸ satisfactory coverage ▸ logical ordering of paragraphs ▸ attempts to adapt style to purpose/audience	**D** (2–3 marks) ▸ sentences are varied ▸ some control of a range of punctuation ▸ spelling of commonly used words is usually accurate ▸ control of tense and agreement is generally secure.

Higher — WJEC GCSE English and English Language

2.14 Sample responses

Here are two reports from students in response to the exam task below. Read the answers and explain the key differences between them.

As secretary of your youth club, you have been asked to write a report on facilities for young children and teenagers in your area. Write what you would say. (20 marks)

Student 1 – Grade C

Report re. activities for teenagers in the local community

Introduction

To collect information I have conducted surveys in many different forms and have come across some common opinions. I have asked people at my local youth club to fill in questionnaires of which I have recieved about 20 completed and I have also spoken to about 10 people in person.

Findings

Many of the local youth club seem to spend their evenings in the children's play park which, in my opinion, is unfair on the young children whom this park is aimed at if they were to graffiti it or break parts of it. They all complained that there were not many places to meet new people and that once you had made friends there were few places to 'hang about' with them. Many said they would like to see more activities to engage in during the day such as a sports centre and a way to spend time together without the general public assuming they were in gangs and are going to attack people.

Recommendations

I understand that you have many other things to think about at this time but I honestly believe small changes could make a big difference to the children of tomorrow. I suggest that a small sports centre would be good with many organised activities to entertain youth during the day. I would also think that a skate park would be a great area to 'hang out'. It would keep them from annoying other people and could be an area a little away from the residential areas where teenagers could make noise as well as graffiting and decorating in any way they see fit.

Conclusion

I would like to stress how much I appriciate you taking the time out of your busy schedule to read this but this is a very important issue and could have a positive impact on our community.

Worksheet 2.14

Higher — WJEC GCSE English and English Language

Student 2 – Grade A

Bridport's facilities for young children and teenagers

Introduction

As secretary of the local youth club I have compiled a report on the local facilities for teenagers and young children. I have compiled data through talking with fellow teenagers living in the area and this is an overview of my findings and possible solutions.

Findings

After speaking with various teenagers I found the following things:

1 Teenagers feel that there isn't anywhere they can go with there friends unless they socialise where there are too many younger children e.g. at the youth club where there are 'too many primary school children shouting and screaming'.

2 Also those who do go to the youth centre find it increasingly dull and in desperate need of modernisation.

3 Furthermore the skate park and football fields are always crowded with 'intimidating individuals' and the feeling is that they are unapproachable, especially to girls and females generally who dislike the damaged and littered area.

4 The skate park is 'too far off the beaten track' and is outside the town so too far away from other people.

5 There aren't any clubs where teenagers and younger adults can meet up to socialise.

6 There is no sports hall where parties and other events can be held.

Possible Solutions

The problem about the youth club would be solved by simply refurbishing the centre and making it more accessible to people of our age. My solution to the other problem concerning our youth centre would be to dedicate certain days of the week and events exclusively to the teenage community.

As in the nearby town of Dorchester, I would suggest that a new more central skate park is created because as has been proved there it encourages co-operation, bonding and friendship as well as a fun environment to enjoy. This could also solve the problem of the park being too far off the beaten path whilst also discouraging the poor behaviour some individuals feel they can get away with because they are too far away from authoritative figures.

Older teenagers have had to travel as far as Sidmouth to go to clubs for younger people and this has meant that they have had an awful lot of trouble getting to and from this location. A solution could be to invest some money in having a council owned building so that they can go to somewhere closer and it could also be a significant money earner too.

Furthermore a newly developed sports and leisure centre would be a perfect solution and benefit all ages of the local community.

In conclusion I would like to thank you on behalf of all teenagers and adolescents in our area for letting our voice be heard amongst those who can make a real difference for us. I hope you will take all my findings into consideration because they will surely improve the facilities in the area for everyone.

© Pearson Education Limited 2010

Worksheet 2.14

Writing articles for magazines and newspapers
Teaching and learning and GradeStudio

Learning Objectives
- to understand the features of an article
- to understand what makes an article effective

Required resources
- Student Book, pages 122–125
- a selection of magazines and newspapers
- Worksheet 2.15: Key features of articles
- Worksheet 2.16: The structure of an article
- Worksheet 2.17: Language choices in articles

Assessment Objectives
Write clearly, effectively and imaginatively, using and adapting forms and selecting vocabulary appropriate to task and purpose in ways which engage the reader (English AO3i; English Language AO4i)

1 Starter
Distribute a selection of magazines and newspapers (or specific articles). Distribute copies of **Worksheet 2.15** and explain the task, using the instructions on the worksheet. Students complete task 1 in pairs. After 15 minutes, ask volunteers to share some of their findings.

Students complete task 2 independently. After 3 minutes, take feedback to consolidate and ensure understanding.

Taking suggestions from around the room, complete task 3, creating a checklist of key ideas on the board.

2 Whole-class/paired work
Turn to page 122 of the Student Book. Students read the information about articles in the table in Activity 1, and make notes about any aspects of articles that they had not considered during the Starter activity.

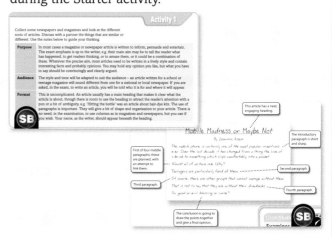

Distribute copies of **Worksheet 2.16**, which contains a jumbled-up version of the article outline on page 123 of the Student Book. Explain the task, using the instructions on the worksheet. Pairs spend 3–5 minutes working on task 1, then check their answers against page 123 of the Student Book.

Taking suggestions from around the room, complete task 2 on the worksheet, adding to the checklist of key ideas on the board.

3 Whole-class/paired work

Introduce the student responses on pages 124–125. Explain that as students now have an understanding of the structure of an article, they need to consider language choices closely.

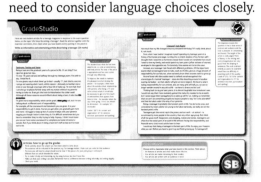

Distribute copies of **Worksheet 2.17**, which looks at the language choices used in the two GradeStudio responses. Explain the task, using the instructions on the worksheet. Pairs spend 5–7 minutes working on task 1.

Taking suggestions from around the room, complete task 2 on the worksheet, adding to the checklist of key ideas on the board.

4 Interactive GradeStudio

Open the interactive GradeStudio activity using ActiveTeach.

The objective of this activity is to help students self-assess their work against the mark scheme and to identify how to achieve higher marks.

This activity is an opportunity for students to assess their own work with the examiner's help. It is suited to students working independently at a computer rather than the whole class. Students can time themselves typing an answer to the set question or they can paste in an answer they have already written to the question.

When they have finished writing, they choose the grade they think they have achieved from the mark scheme. The examiner helps them to check whether they have reached this grade with a series of questions.

Finally, the student can rework their answer with the feedback, or print it out for the teacher to check. The answer they have written can also be saved.

5 Plenary

Students now put all these ideas together to plan their own response to one of the article tasks they have looked at today. After 5 minutes, students swap plans with a partner and check that their partner's plan shows awareness of the need for the right features, structure and language.

Ask: What is the most important aspect of article writing you should remember for the exam?

6 Further work

For homework, ask students to demonstrate their understanding of articles by writing a response to the task featured in Activity 2 on page 123 of the Student Book:

Your local newspaper is running a series of articles on subjects of interest to teenagers. You have been asked to contribute an article on: Mobile phones, a blessing or a curse?

Writing articles for magazines and newspapers
Exam practice and assessment

Learning Objectives
- to practise using key features of an article
- to develop a secure approach to writing an article

Required resources
- Student Book, pages 126–127
- Worksheet 2.18: Exam tasks
- Worksheet 2.19: Board annotation comments

Assessment Objectives
Write clearly, effectively and imaginatively, using and adapting forms and selecting vocabulary appropriate to task and purpose in ways which engage the reader (English AO3i; English Language AO4i)

1 Starter

Distribute copies of **Worksheet 2.18** and explain the tasks, using the instructions on the worksheet. Students work in pairs to complete the tasks. Using ActiveTeach, display the worksheet.

After 10 minutes, take feedback from students, and use their ideas to complete the grid. Students recap the key features of article writing.

2 Whole-class/paired work

Explain that technical accuracy, effective organisation, and sustaining the appropriate tone for purpose and audience, are all essential parts of writing successful articles.

Using ActiveTeach, display the student response on page 124 of the Student Book.

Read the first paragraph of the response to the class. Ask students to identify a strength and a weakness in it (e.g. weakness: 'Being a teen are' – mixed tenses; strength: 'Or are they?' – informal rhetorical question is a good style choice for audience and purpose).

Read the rest of the article to continue to gain a sense of the strengths and the weaknesses throughout it.

Explain that students now need to focus on one area of strength or weakness and find an example of it in the response.

Distribute the 'board annotation comments' on **Worksheet 2.19** around the room.

Explain that these will be stuck around the article to indicate where the particular strength or weakness occurs.

In pairs students should discuss where their comment could be placed. After 3 minutes, pairs should stick their comments to the board in the appropriate place. Encourage detailed explanations of their choices.

Ask students to reflect on the key things to remember about successful article writing.

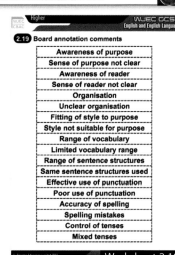

3 Independent work

Introduce Activity 1 on page 126 of the Student Book. Students should read the article and use the mark scheme on page 127 to assess it.

After 5 minutes, take feedback.

Write an article for a travel magazine based on a place you have visited and found interesting. (20 marks)

First of all, Cuba. Everyone gets the pronunciation wrong so don't worry if you do first time. It's not 'Queue-ba' its 'Koo-ba'. 'Koo-ba' is the most unspoilt island in the Caribbean. The isolation which followed the revolution of 1958 meant that, for a long time, few visitors ever went there.

My first stop was the city of Havana and one of its most famous hotels – Hotel Nacional. The twin towered hotel has been visited by such diverse characters as Winston Churchill and Robert Plant. The downstairs bar has an interesting collection of photos of celebrities who have stayed there. The hotel fell on hard times but was renovated in the 1990s and is now one of the capital's best.

My first sightseeing trip was to the 'Catedral de la Habana' which dominates a delightful square in the heart of old Havana and is a striking and almost over elaborate building. The interior, by contrast, is simple and plain apart from the decorative altar. The cathedral is well worth a visit. One of its most interesting features is a coffin which is believed to hold the remains of Christopher Columbus. After leaving the cathedral I wandered a short way and found myself in a flea market held from Tuesday to Sunday. A wonderful sight with bright colours and the sound of Cuban music, there was a surprising amount of objects for sale – and most were hand made.

Another must see is the 'Museo de la Revolucion'. The building has been described as looking like a wedding cake. You either love it or loathe its over-the-topness. Impossible to view everything in one visit, there are items that should not be missed, including: Che Guevara's black beret, Fidel Castro's trousers and much more.

A memorable moment for me was taking a trip in a horse and cart. Like all Cubans the driver was a cheerful and chatty man. He showed us a garage full of 1950s cars in excellent condition. In addition, no visit would be complete without a short trip in a unique three seated yellow Cuban taxi. Possibly a little on the unsafe side with no seat belts and the risk of falling out, but a very unforgettable experience.

A highlight of my time in Havana was a visit to the 'Buena Vista Club', an assortment of musicians who played in the concert hall next to the Hotel Nacional.

After five exhilarating days in Havana I travelled to the Varadero Peninsula to stay in a beach hotel. This proved very relaxing with some special features, though it was not the same 'flavour' as the real Cuba. Having said that our hotel was ideal. With the beach on the doorstep and a bar in the pool, it's the perfect place to relax and enjoy the sun.

Cuba has left a lasting impression on me – the colours and sounds were so vivid. It was so fascinating to see a society which is so different from our own.

Activity 1

Although this is not the complete article, there is enough here to judge its quality. If you were the examiner, what mark would you award for this article? Remember that the mark of 20 is split between content and organisation (13) and sentence structure, punctuation and spelling (7). Use the mark scheme opposite to help your judgement.

SB

Introduce Activity 2 on page 127 of the Student Book. Students now independently write their articles, then use the Peer/Self-assessment questions to check their work.

Activity 2

Now write your own article, using this question set in the exam.

Write an article for a primary school newspaper in which you [tell] Year 6 class what life is like in your secondary school. [marks)]

SB

Peer/Self-assessment

1 Check your answers to Activity 2.
- Did you set out your article appropriately?
- Is there a catchy heading?
- Has it been paragraphed?
- Does the introduction engage the reader?
- Are the central paragraphs clearly organised?
- Is the article rounded off with a short conclusion?
- Does it sound like a primary school newspaper article for Year 6?
- Are you happy with the level of clarity and accuracy?

2 Now try to grade your answer to Activity 2 using the mark scheme below. You will need to be careful and precise in your marking.

4 Plenary

Students swap their articles with a partner, then use the mark scheme on page 127 of the Student Book to grade their peer's response. They should annotate the response where they can see aspects of the mark scheme being fulfilled. They should also make any suggestions for improvement.

Ask volunteers to identify a particularly effective feature of their partner's work to feed back to the class. Hear students' examples, encouraging developed explanations as to why each feature is effective.

5 Further work

For homework, students find an article on the internet and annotate it, identifying the similarities and differences between this kind of article and those found in magazines and newspapers.

Suggested answers

Activity 1, page 126

This is A* work: 13/13 and 7/7 i.e. full marks.

If we look at the A-grade descriptors, we see that the work comfortably meets those requirements. There is sophisticated understanding of the purpose of the task, sustained awareness of the reader, detailed coverage, good selection of detail, effective paragraphing, a range of stylistic devices, and ambitious vocabulary. Since the piece displays all of these, the mark will be at the top of the band.

The SSPS mark scheme mentions variety of sentence structures, accurate punctuation confidently used, accurate spelling, tense control, etc. Again, there is assurance in all the aspects indicated above. The article is virtually error free.

2.5 Leaflets

Writing leaflets

Learning Objectives

- to understand what makes a leaflet a distinctive publication
- to understand how to make a leaflet effective

Required resources

- Student Book, pages 128–133
- A range of leaflets
- Worksheet 2.21: Analysing leaflets
- Worksheet 2.22: Improving a B-grade response
- Worksheet 2.23: Leaflet success questions
- Worksheet 2.24: Peer/Self-assessment
- Worksheet 2.25: Analysing leaflets – suggested answers

Assessment Objectives

Write clearly, effectively and imaginatively, using and adapting forms and selecting vocabulary appropriate to task and purpose in ways which engage the reader (English AO3i; English Language AO4i)

1 Starter

Distribute two or three leaflets to the students. Pairs of students should list the features that make the leaflets different from other non-fiction texts. After 5 minutes, take feedback and establish a class checklist of key features of a leaflet.

2 Whole-class/paired work

Turn to page 128 of the Student Book and read the introductory information about leaflets. Introduce Activity 1 and read the extract from the Recycling leaflet on page 129. Distribute copies of **Worksheet 2.21**, and display the leaflet using ActiveTeach.

With students, identify the answer to the first question for Activity 1. Students record this answer on the table on their worksheets, then work in pairs to analyse the rest of the leaflet and answer the remaining questions.

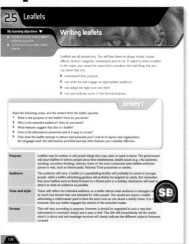

3 Independent work

Introduce the leaflet written by a student on page 130 of the Student Book. Students read the student response and the examiner comments. After 5 minutes, ask students to sum up the key things that the examiner is looking for in this task. Add to the checklist on the board.

Distribute copies of **Worksheet 2.22**. Using the examiner comments as a guide, students try to improve the B-grade response on the worksheet. After 10 minutes, students swap responses with a partner.

Encourage students to share examples of improved responses, ensuring that they explain how the response has been improved and why this has made a difference.

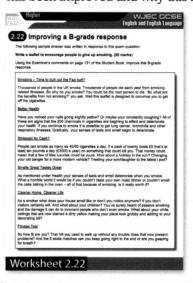

Starter
- **Talk partners**: ensure EAL students are paired with strong English speakers. Clarify any difficult language.

Whole-class/paired work
- **Active listening**: read aloud around the class the text on writing leaflets on page 128.

- Make sub-cards of features of leaflets (purpose, audience, tone and style and format) for the **word wall**.
- Produce one leaflet text as a **cloze** with key words deleted, e.g. in the recycling leaflet delete 'odour' and discuss the reasons for the choice.

Development: independent work
Clarify any difficult words in the examiner comment and tip, 'how to go up grades' and 'Putting it into practice' on page 131 such as 'startling', 'uncomfortable facts', 'specific' and the Peer/self assessment on page 133.

4 Plenary

Turn to page 132 of the Student Book. Using ActiveTeach, display the student leaflet.

Cut up a copy of **Worksheet 2.23** and distribute one 'leaflet success question' to each pair. Pairs should use their question to assess how successful the leaflet is, and write their comments on the back of the question, making sure they explain their ideas fully.

After 5 minutes, pairs feed back their findings by explaining their question and their answer, then sticking their 'leaflet success question' in an appropriate place around the answer on the board.

Worksheet 2.23

5 Further work

For homework, students complete the leaflet task outlined in Activity 4 on page 133 of the Student Book. They should first research any new theme parks that have just opened/are about to open, or brainstorm ideas for a new theme park. Distribute copies of **Worksheet 2.24** for students to complete once they have written their leaflets.

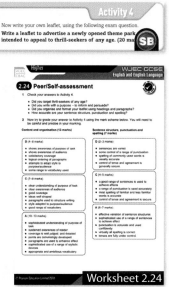

Worksheet 2.24

Suggested answers

Activity 1, page 128
Suggested answers are provided on Worksheet 2.25.

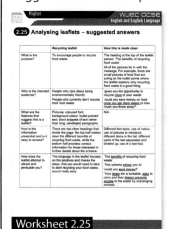

Worksheet 2.25

Writing a speech or talk
Teaching and Learning and GradeStudio

Learning Objectives
- to explore what makes a good speech
- to learn how to construct a speech.

Required resources
- Student Book, pages 134–137
- Video clip 2.2: Tony Blair delivering a speech
- Worksheet 2.26: What's in a speech?
- Worksheet 2.27: Speech transcript
- Worksheet 2.28: Banished to Room 101!

Assessment Objectives
Write clearly, effectively and imaginatively, using and adapting forms and selecting vocabulary appropriate to task and purpose in ways which engage the reader (English AO3i; English Language AO4i)

1 Starter

Distribute copies of **Worksheet 2.26** and read the information about speeches with the class. Ask students to think of speeches they have listened to (or use the examples suggested in Activity 1 on page 134 of the Student Book). Students consider which speech techniques they can remember being used in those speeches, and what effect they had on them.

Distribute copies of **Worksheet 2.27**, which is a transcript of Tony Blair's speech. Students highlight the parts of the text that make it clear that this is from a speech.

Using ActiveTeach, students watch **Video clip 2.2** of Tony Blair's speech, underlining the parts of the speech that they find most engaging. After watching the clip, give students 3 minutes to attach explanations saying why they found specific parts engaging.

Take feedback, encouraging students to consider and explain how the speech has been made engaging.

Worksheet 2.26

Worksheet 2.27

Video 2.2

2 Whole-class/paired work

Turn to page 134 of the Student Book and read the information about speech-writing.

Writing a speech
If you are asked to write a speech in the exam, you will be informed of its intended audience and purpose.

Purpose	Speeches might be to give information, to explain/argue a point of view and perhaps, to persuade. The emphasis will be different depending on the precise circumstances. A politician's emphasis will be on persuasion, while a scientist might concentrate on giving information and raising issues.
Audience	In the exam this will be made clear to you; it is a vital piece of information. The content and style of a speech for younger children will be very different from a speech intended for the governing body of your school or a group of local business people.
Tone	This again will be influenced by audience and circumstances. If you are talking to your classmates, it may be less formal and more chatty than if you are addressing adults. If it is a contribution to a phone-in, it w probably be less formal.

Introduce Activity 2 on page 135 of the Student Book.

Activity 2

1 Using the guidelines for planning and writing a speech below, write a speech in response to the following question set for the exam.
For your Speaking and Listening assessment for GCSE English, you have been asked to address your class on the topic 'Things I would happily put in Room 101'. Try to be entertaining and explain why you would want to get rid of the things you hate. (20 marks)

2 Compare your answer to those in GradeStudio on pages 136–137. Which one is your speech closest to? How could you improve your speech?

Distribute copies of **Worksheet 2.28**, which helps students to generate ideas and plan their answer for Activity 2, task 1. Explain the tasks, using the instructions on the worksheet. Students complete task 1, working in groups to generate plenty of ideas. After 5 minutes, students complete task 2 in pairs. After 5–7 minutes, take feedback to allow students to share their ideas.

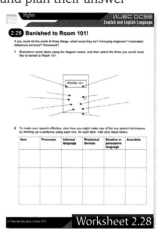
Worksheet 2.28

Starter
- Clarify 'engage' with **message abundancy** and any cultural or idiomatic words.
- **Sentence starters** for explaining and commenting could be given for support.

Whole-class/paired work
- **Active listening**: teacher or a very capable English speaker should read the Grade C answer on page 136 in the Student Book (and the A* answer on page 137) clearly, with expression and appropriate pauses, facial expression and gestures. Encourage EAL students to

highlight text they don't understand while you read and use **talk partners** or **whole-class discussion** to clarify cultural vocabulary and language issues.
- Clarify vocabulary in the examiner summaries and peer/self assessments.

N.B. Many EAL students are unlikely to know all, if any, of the TV programmes and celebrities mentioned so you may need to explain what they are about through a class discussion **sharing prior knowledge**.

The Moving up grades box could be made into a **dictogloss** which will provide the students with clear stages to follow in the speech writing process which they could memorise.

3 Independent work

Using the guidance on page 135 of the Student Book, students write their speeches for Activity 2. Check that they have made use of different speech techniques, and that their structure matches the outline on page 135 of the Student Book.

4 Plenary

Students read the sample responses in GradeStudio, on pages 136–137 of the Student Book, then compare their own speech to the samples provided and assess what grade they are working at.

Students identify a target for themselves for improving their speech-writing.

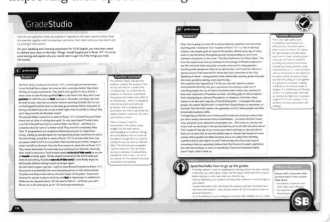

5 Interactive GradeStudio

Open the interactive GradeStudio activity using ActiveTeach.

The objective of this activity is to help students self-assess their work against the mark scheme and to identify how to achieve higher marks.

This activity is an opportunity for students to assess their own work with the examiner's help. It is suited to students working independently at a computer rather than the whole class. Students can time themselves typing an answer to the set question or they can paste in an answer they have already written to the question.

When they have finished writing, they choose the grade they think they have achieved from the mark scheme. The examiner helps them to check whether they have reached this grade with a series of questions.

Finally, the student can rework their answer with the feedback or print it out for the teacher to check. The answer they have written can also be saved.

6 Further work

For homework, students find one of the following famous speeches: Abraham Lincoln's 'Gettysburg Address', Winston Churchill's 'We will fight them on the beaches', Martin Luther King's 'I have a dream', Nelson Mandela's 'An ideal for which I am prepared to die' or Earl Spencer's speech at Princess Diana's funeral. Students should analyse the techniques that make these speeches effective. They should also consider why these speeches continue to have such an impact.

Writing a speech or talk

Exam practice and assessment

Learning Objectives
- to practise using key features of writing a speech
- to develop a secure approach to writing a speech

Required resources
- Student Book, pages 138–139
- Worksheet 2.29: Sample speech
- Worksheet 2.30: Analysing the success questions

Assessment Objectives
Write clearly, effectively and imaginatively, using and adapting forms and selecting vocabulary appropriate to task and purpose in ways which engage the reader (English AO3i; English Language AO4i)

1 Starter

Ask students to recap the different speech techniques established in the previous lesson.

Distribute copies of **Worksheet 2.29**, which contains the speech from page 138 of the Student Book. Students highlight examples of speech techniques in the sample response. Take feedback to consolidate and ensure understanding.

2 Whole-class/paired work

Using ActiveTeach, display **Worksheet 2.30**. Explain that students are going to analyse how successfully the student on page 138 has fulfilled the task.

Using the questions to guide them, students analyse and annotate the sample response with their ideas. Take feedback to consolidate and ensure understanding. Encourage students to identify specific examples from the speech to illustrate their analysis. Establish a class checklist of key things to remember to complete this task successfully.

Starter
- **Clarify** 'engage' with **message abundancy** and any cultural or idiomatic words used in the videos.
- **Sentence starters** for explaining and commenting could be given for support.

Whole class/paired work
- Encourage EAL students to **highlight text** they don't understand while you read and use **talk partners** or **whole class discussion** to clarify cultural vocabulary

and language issues such as: 'come on', 'and all', 'like to fancy', 'div', 'lame' and the celebrities listed.
- **Also clarify** vocabulary in the examiner summaries and peer/self assessments such as: 'provocative', 'fluently', 'acknowledging', 'dramatic effect', 'awkwardness', 'controversial', 'witty', 'sophisticated'.
- Be aware that many EAL students are unlikely to know all, if any, of the TV programmes and celebrities mentioned so you may need to **explain** what they are about though a class discussion **sharing prior knowledge**.

3 Independent work

Introduce Activity 2 on page 139 of the Student Book. Students write their speeches, then use the Peer/Self-assessment questions to check their work.

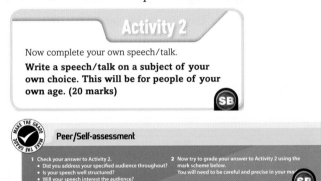

Suggested answers

Activity 1, page 139
This is an A* response.

The student has been asked to write a speech for a very specific audience. She demonstrates excellent understanding of the purpose of the task (to inform, explain, and to reassure), register, tone etc. There is a sustained awareness of the audience (11 year olds). Coverage is well judged and detailed. The work is well paragraphed and well organised and vocabulary is used in an assured and appropriate way. Sentences are varied and constructed with the audience in mind. There is the injection of the occasional short sentence for effect – 'You will', 'It really helps'. A range of punctuation is used and used effectively and correctly – apostrophes, exclamation marks, commas etc. Spelling is accurate. In fact, the piece is virtually error free.

4 Plenary

Students swap speeches with a partner and use the mark scheme on page 139 of the Student Book to grade their partner's response. They should annotate the response where they can see aspects of the mark scheme being fulfilled. They should also make any suggestions for improvement.

Ask volunteers to identify any particularly effective features of their partner's work to feed back to the class. Hear students' examples, encouraging developed explanations as to why each feature is effective.

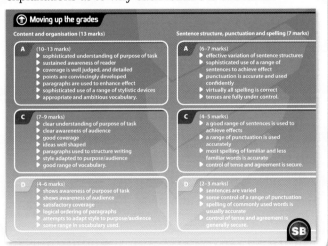

Writing a review

Learning Objective
- to learn about writing reviews, in particular of books, films and music

Required resources
- Student Book, pages 140–145
- Video clip 2.3: *The Culture Show*
- Worksheet 2.31: Review writing
- Worksheet 2.32: Sample music reviews
- Worksheet 2.33: Sample film reviews
- Worksheet 2.34: Review writing – suggested answers
- Worksheet 2.35: Writing a review – suggested answers

Assessment Objectives
Write clearly, effectively and imaginatively, using and adapting forms and selecting vocabulary appropriate to task and purpose in ways which engage the reader (English AO3i; English Language AO4i)

1 Starter

Worksheet 2.31

Distribute copies of **Worksheet 2.31** and use the explanation notes on the worksheet to introduce the task. Using ActiveTeach, students watch **Video clip 2.3**, making notes on their worksheets. Take feedback, asking students to identify parts of the review that were particularly effective in making the reviewer's opinions clear. Encourage detailed explanations as to why. Suggested answers are provided on **Worksheet 2.34**.

Introduce Activity 1 on page 140 of the Student Book. Ask students to think of a book, film or CD they have recently come across. Give them 3 minutes to begin a review for that item. Hear some examples. Students attempt to identify their peer's opinion of the item.

Activity 1
Think about the last book you read, the last film you watched, the last CD you listened to. Explain what you thought of it, then write your notes below.

Video 2.3

2 Whole-class/paired work

Turn to page 140 of the Student Book and read the explanations about reviews and their purpose, format and audience.

Introduce Activity 2 on page 141. Students read the three reviews and discuss in pairs what features the reviews have in common. After 5–7 minutes, take feedback and use students' ideas to generate a class checklist of key features of reviews.

3 Group work

Introduce the sample responses in GradeStudio, on pages 142–143 of the Student Book. Students should read the responses and the examiner's comments. Ask students to summarise what they think examiners are looking for in a successful review.

Organise the class into groups of four students. Allocate a pair in each group, one of two questions to focus on:

Write a review of a music album with which you are familiar.

Write a review of a film which you have recently seen.

Distribute the appropriate worksheet to each pair.
Worksheet 2.32 contains sample music reviews and **Worksheet 2.33** contains sample film reviews. Using the instructions on the worksheet, explain the task.

Worksheet 2.32

After 10 minutes, pairs should feed back their findings to the rest of the group.

Ask students to reflect on what this has shown them about effective review-writing.

Worksheet 2.33

4 Interactive GradeStudio

Open the interactive GradeStudio activity using ActiveTeach.

The objective of this activity is to understand what skills are required at different grades, and that there are different ways to achieve the same grade. This activity gives a range of sample answers for each grade.

At the front of the class analyse and compare the answers to the same grade, and compare the answer at different grades.

Discuss the examiner comments with the class so that students can understand what skills are required at each grade and see that there are different ways to achieve the same grade.

Students will become familiar with the criteria specific to each grade. Students will also be shown the best way to arrive at that grade. In addition, by comparing answers to the same question the students can see how questions are commonly misinterpreted and marks are lost.

5 Independent work

Turn to the exam practice section on pages 144–145 of the Student Book. Students read the example review on page 144, then complete Activity 3.

Ask students to reflect on common weaknesses that occur in review-writing, and to suggest effective strategies to overcome them.

6 Further work

For homework, students write a response to Activity 4 on page 145 of the Student Book. They should complete the review and attempt to mark their own work, using the understanding they have developed in today's lesson.

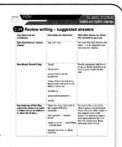

Suggested answers

Suggested answers for Worksheet 2.31

Suggested answers are provided on **Worksheet 2.34**.

Activity 2, page 141; Activity 3, page 144

Suggested answers for the above activities are provided in **Worksheet 2.35**.

Making a recording

Learning Objectives
- to understand how to record spoken language effectively
- to make a record of spoken language

Required resources
- Student Book, pages 152–153
- Worksheet 4.1: Making a recording – Starter
- Worksheet 4.2: Making a recording – Development
- Worksheet 4.3: making a recording – Notes

Assessment Objectives
- Understand variations in spoken language, explaining why language changes in relation to contexts
- Evaluate the impact of spoken language choices in their own and others' use

(English language AO2i and ii)

1 Starter

Read aloud the excerpt from the Tom Leonard poem on **Worksheet 4.1** in your best Glasgow accent. Give pairs 10 minutes to complete the two questions on the worksheet.

Explain that this kind of writing is called 'eye-dialect'. It is sometimes used to try to convey aspects of speech, particularly accent. It tends to be used in jokes and sometimes in literature, but you have to know the accent before you can understand it (e.g. kangaroot = Geordie stuck in a lift).

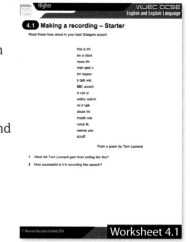

2 Independent work

Allow 35 minutes for students to complete Task 1 of Activity 1 on page 152 of the Student Book. They will make a recording (no more than 1 minute in total) using one of the following:
- mobile phone with recording function
- laptop and microphone
- cassette player or reel-to-reel tape recorder
- television, and dvd or video player
- a computer (and YouTube or VideoJug) to make a written recording.

Suggestions for what students may record:
- conversation (but not more than three or four people speaking at a time)
- live commentary on TV (e.g. sports commentary, panel comments on *Strictly Come Dancing*, *Britain's Got Talent, Have I Got News for You*)
- live radio – phone-ins, chat shows but **not** scripted speech such as the news
- pre-recorded material on Youtube (e.g. Stephen Fry being interviewed on *Parkinson*, a Barack Obama interview or Johnathon Ross's interviews) but **not** scripted or polished material such as comedy routines or set-piece speeches.

Students can use pre-recorded material as long as the spoken language is spontaneous and not scripted, rehearsed or edited. Interviews and interactive speech are safest, for example chat shows but not the news; band interviews or radio phone-ins but not soap operas. Vox pops, post-match interviews, comments from judges or performers on shows such as *Strictly Come Dancing* are fine. Planned, scripted or edited material **can** work for the study of language variation, as it is more focused on attitudes towards the standard or non-standard language (for more detail see page 109).

3

Students should check their recording from Activity 1 against the checklist on page 152 of the Student Book.

Students should then complete Task 3 of Activity 1, using the table on **Worksheet 4.2** to evaluate what went well and what could be improved.

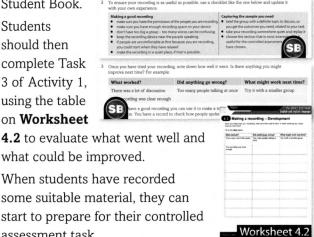

Worksheet 4.2

When students have recorded some suitable material, they can start to prepare for their controlled assessment task.

Questions your students might usefully ask themselves as they fill in **Worksheet 4.2**:
- Am I using the right kind of recording device?
- Have I put my microphone in the right place?
- Is my group too big or too small?
- Are my speakers relaxed and speaking naturally?
- Have they got something interesting to talk about?
- Do I want to/need to join in the conversation?
- Shall I record one, two or more examples?
- Do I have enough details of who was speaking and where and when the recording took place?
- When I have completed my recording(s) do I need to transcribe them?

Introduce Activity 2 on page 153 of the Student Book. Students should be aware that note-making can be done quickly and easily in a notebook or even using the memo facility on a mobile phone.

Distribute or display **Worksheet 4.3** to help students with Activity 2.

Worksheet 4.3

4 Plenary

Pairs discuss what is lost and gained by each method of recording. Give them 5 minutes to do this. Consolidate the discussion as a whole class for a further 5 minutes.

5 Further work

Ask students to replay one of their recordings from Activity 1. This time they record the information in note form. Once they have done this, students should ask themselves the following:
- Which worked best here – the notes or the recording?
- Which was quicker and easier?
- Which way of working did I prefer?
- Is it necessary to transcribe everything? (Note: sometimes it is.)
- Which method will I use for my controlled assessment?

Suggested answers

Starter

1 What did Tom Leonard gain from writing like this?

Likely responses will include the following, though will not necessarily using these words, which you might begin to introduce now.
- he comments on the idea of two kinds of language – BBC language and the voice of 'wanna yoo scruff'
- the short lines break up the idea of sentences and become more speech-like
- the sounds of speech with an accent – n, coz, yoo, widny, scruff, aboot, trooth, wia
- stress and emphasis on certain words
- the natural repetition we get in speech
- pace – from the short lines
- dialect – scruff, widny (would not).

2 How successful is it in sounding like speech? Successful if you've heard a Glasgow accent!

Using transcripts

Learning Objectives

- to understand some key features of a transcript
- to make a transcript

Required resources

- Student Book, pages 154–155
- Worksheet 4.4: Using transcript – Starter
- Worksheet 4.5: Using transcripts – Key transcript symbols
- Worksheet 4.6: Using transcripts
- Worksheet 4.7: Using transcripts – Further work

Assessment objectives

- Understand variations in spoken language, explaining why language changes in relation to contexts
- Evaluate the impact of spoken language choices in their own and others' use.

(English language AO2i and ii)

1 Starter

Distribute **Worksheet 4.4**. Ask students, in pairs, to act out the transcript on the worksheet, using the symbols table on the sheet to help them. The transcript is taken from Activity 1 on page 154 of the Student Book.

Worksheet 4.4

2 Whole-class work

Using ActiveTeach, display the two representations of the shop scene on page 154 of the Student Book: the transcript and the standard written version. Ask students for their responses to the question in Activity 1: 'What do you learn from the transcript that you don't get in the standard written version'? Points to establish with the class are: how important the pauses are; the shopkeeper's irritation at being interrupted; and the stress on the underlined words. It's much more difficult to show these features in a 'written' version.

Students split into pairs to complete Activity 2 on page 154, using the explanation of key transcript symbols on **Worksheet 4.5**. When students start to turn a part of their recordings into a transcript, the tips on this worksheet might prove useful.

Worksheet 4.5

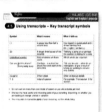

Activity 3 will give students more familiarity with transcript symbols before they start to make their own transcripts for their controlled assessment task.

Once students have a transcript, they can add notes to it, or highlight features (see **Worksheet 4.6**) that will help in the controlled assessment task. Students are allowed to take transcripts into the controlled assessment task.

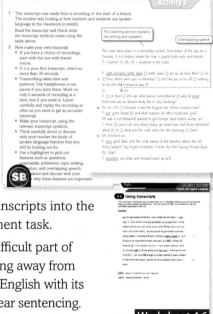

Worksheet 4.6

Usually the most difficult part of transcribing is getting away from the idea of written English with its punctuation and clear sentencing. Students should be free to add to or limit what they mark on their transcripts. If they wish to use bold for emphasis then fine, there are no set rules. They should use what works. Students shouldn't lose sight of the purpose of a transcript – to represent speech on paper. Recordings can be referred to as well.

A transcript needn't be continuous: students can choose the most fruitful sections to transcribe. Language change and choice tasks benefit from a transcript, variation may be better served with a table or notebook.

Starter/Worksheet 4.3
- **Active listening**: the teacher should read aloud the text in Activity 1, as it is written and then as it would be spoken.
- **Active listening**: opportunities should be provided for EAL students to hear the differences between the two versions of the text.
- Clarify where the vocabulary is stressed, 'regular' and 'two' and the effect this has on the spoken version.
- **Activity 3** page 155 is a **visual presentation** which should aid completion of Worksheet 4.3.

- Clarify key vocabulary as appropriate such as: 'dialect', 'accent', 'effect', 'overlap', 'interrupt', 'emphasis' to consolidate.
- Read through the key transcript symbols page 155 to aid understanding of what each symbol tells us.
- **Active listening**: read the marking task aloud before playing the recording and check understanding. It will need to be played more than once so that students can follow the transcript *and* add in the details.
- After the first reading, use **talk partners** to allow EAL learners to note the standard spellings of as many words as possible.

3 Plenary/Self-assessment
Students self-assess and compare what was the most difficult part of using a transcript. Take feedback and discuss with the class. How much transcribing do they think will be necessary for a language change, choice or variation task?

4 Further work
Distribute copies of **Worksheet 4.7**. Explain the task using the instructions on the worksheet. Play the sound file of the transcript, which can be found at: http://www.bbc.co.uk/voices/recordings/group/bristol-knowlewest.shtml or go to http://www.bbc.co.uk/voices/recordings/, hover over the Bristol area on the map and find the 'Church social club members' dot. Then select 'Voice clip 3'.

Students listen to the clip several times, and then annotate the transcript with the features listed on the worksheet. Discuss with the class, using the summary notes on the worksheet.

Worksheet 4.7

Suggested answers

Activity 2, page 154

No (.) I'm not going to **London** tomorrow
(Meaning: More emphasis on the listener getting it wrong. 'No, (stupid) I'm not going to London, I'm going to Brighton.')

No (2) I'm **not** going to London tomorrow
(Meaning: I'm not going to London and nothing you say can change my mind.)

No (.) I'm not **going** to London tomorrow
(Meaning – No, I'm coming back from London.)

Using spoken language recollection

Learning Objectives

- to understand how to work with spoken language recollection
- to bring together a spoken language recollection

Required resources

- Student Book, pages 156–157
- Video clip 4.1: Spoken language in *Word on the Street*
- Worksheet 4.8: Spoken language in *Word on the Street*
- Worksheet 4.9: Spoken language in *Word on the Street* – suggested answers

- Worksheet 4.10: Using spoken language – Language recollection

Assessment Objectives

- Understand variations in spoken language, explaining why language changes in relation to contexts
- Evaluate the impact of spoken language choices in their own and others' use

(English language AO2i and ii)

1 Starter

Working individually, students write down all the synonyms they can think of for the verb 'to throw', (for example *chuck*, *lob*). Students then work in pairs to combine their responses and build up to a whole-class response. Discuss some of the examples.

2 Whole-class work

Distribute **Worksheet 4.8**. Explain the task using the instructions on the worksheet. Students are going to watch **Video clip 4.1** from *Word on the Street*, which is of three generations of a Leicestershire family. The family are reminiscing and recollecting their spoken language use. The students' task is to summarise how the people in the video speak and why. Using ActiveTeach, play the first few minutes of the video clip. Students watch the clip, read the transcript provided on **Worksheet 4.8**, if needed, and answer the question on the worksheet. Suggested answers are provided on **Worksheet 4.9**.

Video 4.1

Turn to page 156 of the Student Book and read the introductory text. Introduce Activity 1, and ask the students to construct a list of five words to research individually through recollection, using and adding to the suggestions from Activity 1. A preliminary glance at a thesaurus will show the fruitful areas. 'Male', 'female' and 'young person' are other possibilities.

Allow students 10–15 minutes to develop their synonym lists using the suggestions in the Student Book (activities such as group discussion and internet research will work well here).

Activity 1

1 To work with language recollection in a way that helps with your own controlled assessment task, use the activities below.

- Find out what different words/phrases people use to describe how they feel when they are really pleased or really fed up.
- Find out the different words people use to describe a specific item. Choose items that most interest you, or you could try some of the following: friend, bread roll, mid-morning snack, a foolish person, bad tempered, attractive.

2 To build up your use of language recollection:
- talk with your friends and family; notice the phrases they use and make a note of them as quickly as possible afterwards
- discuss words in a group; share and note down words and phrases (working in a group can help you record more information)
- use the Internet, especially if you belong to a social networking site and know people who might use different words/phrases across the country.

Starter:

- **Talk partners:** pair EAL students with fluent English speakers to work on the synonym activity. Encourage the English speaker to give appropriate contexts for using the synonyms found.
- Clarify words from the explanations and contexts as appropriate using **message abundancy**, such as 'recollection', 'categorise', 'location', 'Cockney', 'Geordie', 'cross-over'.

- **ICT-based tools/** Bilingual dictionaries: EAL students could work in pairs with e-thesaurus to find synonyms for 'throw'.
- **Active listening**: the teacher should provide opportunities for EAL students to hear the pronunciation of as many of the words as possible.

Plenary

- **Activate prior knowledge**: the teacher should encourage EAL students to share any of the experiences suggested for a controlled assessment task, especially: 'Me and my language - how I choose to speak to different people in my life.'

3 Homework

For Activity 2, students talk to friends, family members and/or older relatives to investigate variation in spoken language. They use the table on **Worksheet 4.10** to log their findings. (**Worksheet 4.10** will help students to capture the information they need about language recollection to support their controlled assessment task.)

Students can begin to categorise the kinds of variation they are finding, using the headings in bold on page 157.

4 Preparing for the controlled assessment task

Students swap responses to Activity 2 with a partner and begin to assess and check the kinds of variation they are finding. They can use their findings to construct a proposal for a controlled assessment task using language recollection. Suggestions are:

- Language choice: 'Me and my language – how I choose to speak to different people in my life'
- Language change: 'Speaking proper: How my words and accent change in different situations'
- Language variation: 'Speak so I know who you are: How spoken language varies in my world'.

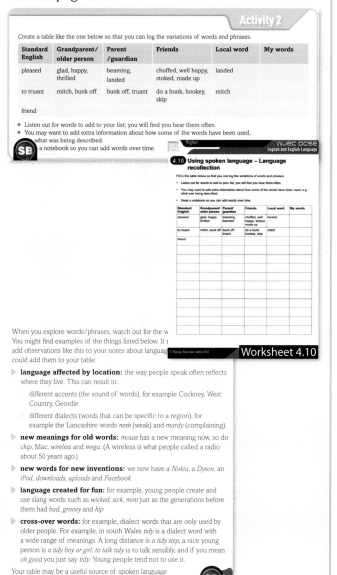

Worksheet 4.10

Suggested answers

Answers for video clip activity

Suggested answers are provided on **Worksheet 4.9**.

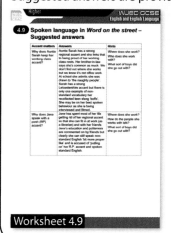

Worksheet 4.9

Language change

Learning Objectives

- to understand how spoken language changes in different contexts
- to analyse a transcript and explain how language changes

Required resources

- Student Book, pages 158–161
- Worksheet 4.11: Language change – Analysing a transcript 1
- Worksheet 4.12: Language change – Analysing a transcript 2

Assessment Objectives

- Understand variations in spoken language, explaining why language changes in relation to contexts
- Evaluate the impact of spoken language choices in their own and others' use.

(English language AO2i and ii)

1 Starter

Split the class into three groups and ask students to think of as many possible questions and contexts as they can that would change the meaning of an answer. For example 'Sorry, no change' could be the answer to several questions including 'Can you break this £5 note down for me?', 'How's your cat, any better?', 'Surely United must be doing better by now'.

The three answers you can use are:

- Sorry, no change.
- Wicked.
- Yes…

Allow 10 minutes for this starter. Write the responses on the board.

3 Independent work

Distribute **Worksheet 4.12**. Ask students to follow the instructions on the worksheet to further explore the transcript. The questions in bold are repeated from page 159 of the Student Book. These questions can be used to explore any language change transcript and recording, in any context. The questions not in bold are more useful for a classroom context.

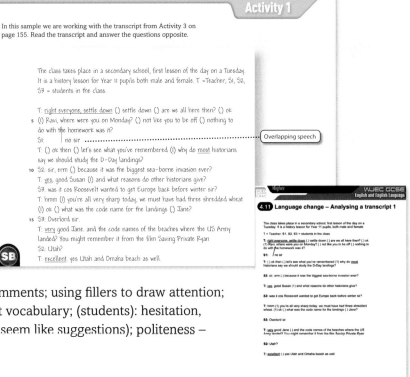

2 Whole-class work

Using ActiveTeach, display the transcript on page 158 of the Student Book and distribute **Worksheet 4.11**, which contains a copy of the transcript.

Role-play the transcript with the students.

Ask students to look at the transcript and consider how teachers and students use spoken language in the classroom. Annotate the transcript with features suggested by the class. Suggested responses are (teacher): use of questions to control the topic and direct activities; giving praise to encourage a positive mood, jokes and light-hearted comments; using fillers to draw attention; adding detail to answers; and use of subject vocabulary; (students): hesitation, shaping answers as questions (makes them seem like suggestions); politeness – frequent use of 'sir'.

Starter:
- **Talk partners**: EAL students and fluent English speakers discuss the change in meaning activity.
- **Activate prior knowledge** of World War II and/or show a **visual presentation** of background information about the D-Day landing as necessary.
- Clarify words as necessary, especially names such as 'Roosevelt', 'Utah' 'Omaha' and the phrase 'we must have had three shredded wheat.'
- Be aware that some EAL students may not have seen *Saving Private Ryan*.

- Be aware also that **pronunciation** difficulties could cause misunderstanding or undermine confidence.
- Clarify any difficult words in the examiner summary, 'how to go up grades' and 'Putting it into practice' – to ensure understanding.
- **Collaborative activities**, GradeStudio: set up pairs or small groups. One lists the spoken language types of features which carry effect; the other finds examples from the transcript and then use both to refine the Grade C answer.

4 Plenary/self-assessment

Students discuss and develop answers to the eight questions in Activity 1 on page 159 of the Student Book. Allow 10 minutes for this task.

Use these questions to explore the transcript opposite. The questions in bold can help you explore language change in any context.

1 **What effect does the situation or context have here?** Classrooms have unwritten rules that everyone follows. Can you suggest some?

2 **Who sets the topic?** How does the teacher signal that the lesson is about to start, and get it going in the right direction?

3 **Which words used here are specific to the subject?** Specialist language is always a feature of language change, for example historical terms such as *historians, sea-borne invasion* and *Roosevelt.*

4 **Who uses questions?** Who uses the most questions in the transcript opposite? Why? Can you find examples of open and closed questions in the transcript opposite?
   - An **open question** is one that can have several different answers and they may be used to generate opinions and start discussion. For example: *Why do most historians say we should study the D-Day landings?*
   - A **closed question** is one that has a short, definite answer, sometimes just yes or no. Closed questions are used to check facts, for example: *What was the code-name for the landings, Jane?*
   - Questions used to control *Are we all here, then?*

5 **Who uses commands and how are they used?**
   - Teachers usually make their commands and their ways of saying 'wrong' polite, e.g. *not quite.* Why do you think that is?
   - Find one polite statement in the transcript opposite that is really an instruction or command.

6 **Pauses are important – what do they say?** Find examples of pauses used by the teacher. Why do you think they have been used?

7 **How do the speakers connect with each other?** Why do you think the teacher uses the word 'we', e.g. *We must have had three shredded wheat?* Why does he say, *You might remember it from the film 'Saving Private Ryan'?*

8 **Who praises?** In a classroom context it is usually the teacher who gives praise. Find two examples of praise in the transcript. Why is praise important? Why does the teacher praise the whole class as well as individuals?

SB

5 Homework – GradeStudio

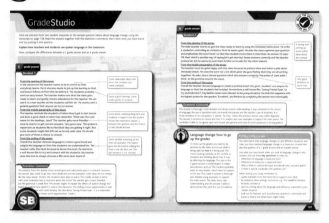

Turn to pages 160–161 of the Student Book where you will find two sample responses, at C-grade and A-grade, for a controlled assessment task. The question for this task is at the top of page 160. Students should write their own response to the question, using the advice in Activity 1 on page 159 of the Student Book.

Students then compare their responses with those on the GradeStudio pages. Using ActiveTeach, display the examiner comments on the whiteboard, so that students can self-assess their answers. (Note: the C-grade response was awarded 12 marks and the A-grade response was awarded 19 marks.)

Suggested answers

Worksheet 4.12

2 The teacher sets the topic by asking a question about the previous lesson

3 Other subject-specific language includes 'get Europe back before winter', 'code name', 'Utah' and 'Omaha and 'D-day landings'.

4 The teacher tends to ask most questions and most closed questions, because he is testing specific information. The students give their answers in question form 'Was it …' to show politeness and uncertainty.

5 The teacher uses commands at the start to establish control.

6 Pauses in line 4 give the class time to be quiet and listen. In line 5 they act as 'punctuation'. The 1-second pause in line 8 could be thinking time or for dramatic effect before the question. In line 10 the hesitation noise and pause seem to be recall time for the right phrase. Line 11 – the pause separates the praise and the next question. Lines 13 and 14: the longer pauses help to emphasise the praise and perhaps signals the teacher thinking 'How can I catch them out?' The pause at the end of line 14 is the 'ask a question, choose a victim' technique.

Language choice

Learning Objectives

- to understand how we choose language for different listeners
- to analyse a transcript and show the significance of language choice

Required resources

- Student Book, pages 162–165
- Worksheet 4.13: Language choice – Starter
- Worksheet 4.14: Language choice – Pauses
- Worksheet 4.15: Language choice – GradeStudio
- Schools should have the 'Inter Group GCSE English Speaking and Listening Training and Guidance DVD' from which the transcript from page 162 of the Student Book is taken, so this could be played if resources permit

Assessment Objectives

- Understand variations in spoken language, explaining why language changes in relationship to contexts
- Evaluate the impact of spoken language choices in their own and others' use.

(English language AO2i and ii)

1 Starter

Distribute **Worksheet 4.13** which contains the 'Keep your head' quiz. Explain the task to the students using the instructions on the worksheet. Student need to correctly match the term of address to the powerful person. Answers are provided in the Suggested answers box.

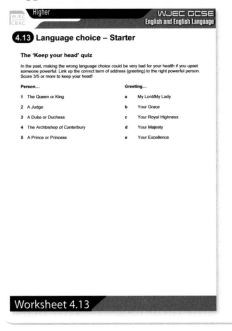

Worksheet 4.13

2 Independent work

Ask students to read the transcript on page 162 of the Student Book. Distribute **worksheet 4.14** and ask the students to complete it. Then introduce Activity 1 on page 163. Allow 20 minutes for students to work individually or in pairs on this activity, answering the six questions.

Worksheet 4.14

The transcript is of an interview between a parent and a headteacher. The parent has brought her son with her; he seems uninterested in the discussion. The headteacher has the administrator with her. It is lunchtime.

Headteacher: (quietly to the administrator) I can tell this parent's going to be a pain (.) try and get some really good facts (.) throw her off ok (3)
Administrator: ok
HT: (very quietly) waste of time. (3) (louder) Miss Lovering (.) hello
5 **Parent:** (to son) sit down (1) I am here today because I am appalled at the standard of food served in your school
HT: well I don't serve any food in this school which is why I've brought my colleague along Alex Bradley-Hooters
Parent: well maybe he can explain then
10 **Administrator:** our food is of high quality from (.) trusted and (.) inspected farmers around the country the food (.) the food is pre-prepared and brought in
Parent: huh
Administrator: in vacuum packs to ensure freshness (1)
HT: there you have it it's absolutely perfect food there's not a problem

Activity 1

Use the questions below to explore the transcript. The questions in bold are useful to explore language choice in any context.

1 **What effects do the language choices of the speakers have?** The language styles of the headteacher are quite different a) when she is talking quietly to the administrator and b) when she is addressing the parent. Pick out two examples of a) non-standard and b) standard language.
2 **Which of the listeners doesn't have to change their style?** Who is adapting their style more, the teacher, the parent or the administrator? Who seems most at ease with the style?
3 **How is the seriousness of the topic signalled by the speakers?** How formal is the parent's language choice here? Choose one or two phrases as examples.
4 **Who uses confident and fluent language?** Often, confident people speak fluently and nervous or unsure people speak hesitantly.
   - Nervous or unsure people pause more often in their speech. Can you find the most nervous person here?
   - How does the parent make it clear that she is less than impressed?
5 **Who uses specialist language?** We can confuse and intimidate people by choosing to use technical language. How does the administrator attempt to impress with jargon? Does he do it well enough to hide his hesitation?
6 **Who decides what is right or wrong?** The headteacher tries to draw the situation to a close by concluding and closing down the discussion. Which of her statements show this most clearly?

3 Whole-class work

Distribute **Worksheet 4.15**, which contains the two sample response on pages 164–165 of the Student Book. Ask students to compare the C-grade answer to the A-grade answer and to identify the main differences.

Using ActiveTeach, display the examiner comments from pages 164–165 of the Student Book, in order to feed back to the students and consolidate understanding.

The main features of the two answers are: the **A-grade** answer – Focuses on what is said but also how it is said, discussing hesitations and pauses. Ideas about the context are subtle and purposefully integrated into the answer. Quotation from the transcript is frequent and supports the main ideas. Formal standard English is identified. The speech behaviour of the son and the administrator receive attention as well as the mother and the head teacher.

The **C-grade** answer is more descriptive and focuses on the purposes of the speech of the administrator, head teacher and mother. To improve the answer some mention of the informal speech 'throw her off ok' would help. Some comment on the choice of vocabulary by the administrator (quite technical and longer words – polysyllabic – would improve the answer.

The A-grade response was awarded 18 marks and the C-grade response was awarded 12 marks.

Worksheet 4.15

4 Plenary/Self-assessment

Recap on the different kinds of pauses and discuss 'Can you always identify the effect or cause of a pause?'

Suggested answers

Starter

1d, 2a, 3b, 4e, 5c

Worksheet 4.14

Three kinds of pauses:
- Punctuation pause – headteacher's first utterance
- Uncertainty pauses – in the speech of the administrator (to the parent)
- Discomfort/disagreement pause – before the administrator replies to the headteacher in line 3

Activity 1, page 163

1 a colloquialisms: 'going to be a pain', 'throw her off'
  b Any examples from the 'public' speech of the headteacher, administrator or parent

2 The administrator's style is least fluent, which suggests uneasiness.

3 The seriousness of the topic is signalled by the formal tone used by all the speakers after the comment 'waste of time'. The parent says 'I am here today...' and 'I am appalled at the standard of food', which initiates a formal tone by using standard English.

4 The headteacher is fluent and confident, the parent has the fluency of anger. The parent's 'Huh' suggests that she is less than impressed.

5 The administrator attempts to impress with jargon ('pre-prepared', 'vacuum packs', 'trusted and inspected farms'). Does this make up for the hesitation? Probably not, but this is a role play by students and there may be different opinions.

6 The headteacher's last utterance tries to close down the discussion.

Language variation

Learning Objectives

- to understand the effects of standard and non-standard spoken language
- to analyse a transcript and demonstrate how standard and non-standard language may vary over time and place

Required resources

- Student Book, pages 166–169
- Worksheet 4.16: Language variation – Starter
- Worksheet 4.17: Language variation – Standard and non-standard forms 1
- Worksheet 4.18: Language variation – Standard and non-standard forms 2

- Worksheet 4.19: Language variation – GradeStudio
- Worksheet 4.20: Language variation – Further work
- Worksheet 4.21: Activity 1 – Suggested answers

Schools should have the 'Inter Group GCSE English Speaking and Listening Training and Guidance' DVD from which the transcripts on page 167 are taken. So this could be played if resources permit.

Assessment Objectives

- Understand variations in spoken language, explaining why language changes in relation to contexts
- Assess the impact of spoken language choices in their own and others' use

(English language AO2i and ii)

1 Starter

Distribute copies of **Worksheet 4.16**, which contains a number of standard and non-standard words. Give students 10 minutes to divide these words into their respective categories on the worksheet.

Worksheet 4.16

2 Whole-class work

Display the two transcripts on page 167 of the Student Book on ActiveTeach, and distribute **Worksheet 4.17**, which contains copies of these transcripts.

Role-play or act out the transcripts.

Collate any comments, notes or observations on the language used. Ask students to then complete the table on page 166, which is provided on **Worksheet 4.18**.

You could ask students to focus on the following:

- the use of non-standard language (dialect) such as 'that were', 'it were'
- accent features – speaking with a local accent
- teen speak – the trendy words teenagers use for 'good' and 'bad'.

Suggested answers are provided on **Worksheet 4.21**.

Worksheet 4.17

Worksheet 4.18

Activity 1

Read the question above and the transcripts opposite. The transcripts show how a speaker has chosen to vary her use of non-standard and standard forms of spoken language in an informal and formal situation. Explore the way the language has been varied by completing a table like the one below.

Non-standard spoken language (to friends)	Standard spoken language (to teacher)	Variation	
it were well good	I had a really good time	Non-standard language including dialect features 'it were' rather than 'it was' and 'well' as an adjective instead of 'really' or 'very'	Local words that define you as coming from a particular place.
they let me 'ave a go at all the jobs	they let me try out all of the jobs	Non-standard language including accent dropping the initial 'h'. Standard language to impress the teacher	Local accent, which is the way you make your sounds. Melissa doesn't sound the 'g' sound in 'hanging' and the 'h' in 'have'. That is accent.
for a coupla days	for two days	Non-standard language, running words together. Informal and probably excited. Standard language to be specific with the teacher	
	I really enjoyed that		
pressie			
	because		
I had a bangin time			

SB

Starter

- **Talk partners**: pair strong English speakers with EAL learners so that EAL learner can learn pronunciation, meanings and uses of the different words in the box.
- Create a **substitution table** of a few sentences including one or more of the adjectives in the starter box and nouns. Discuss how the effect changes if other adjectives and nouns are substituted.

- **Active reading**: it will be beneficial if the teacher reads the introduction to this lesson on page 166, to ensure vocabulary such as 'standard' and 'non-standard', 'formal', 'polite' is understood.

The GradeStudio activities will all be very helpful as – especially the 'important factors'. Revise language features such as 'accent', 'dialect' and the suggestion to use 'may' and 'might', 'could', 'would' and 'should' modal verbs (which are often difficult for EAL learners). **Model** how these words are used several times until the students feel confident in using them.

3 GradeStudio

Turn to pages 168–169 of the Student Book where you will find two sample responses, at C-grade and A-grade, for a controlled assessment task. Alternatively distribute **Worksheet 4.19**, which contains these sample responses.

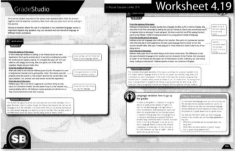

Worksheet 4.19

The question for the controlled assessment task is at the top of page 168. Students should write their own response to the question, and then compare their responses with those on the GradeStudio pages. Using ActiveTeach, display the examiner comments on the whiteboard, so that students can self-assess their answers. (Note: the C-grade response was awarded 13 marks and the A-grade response was awarded 17 marks.)

4 Plenary

Explain to students that as we move around the country and back and forward through time, we constantly find different words and phrases for the same ideas. Ask students: why do we get different words for the same ideas? Discuss the following possibilities.

- People are naturally inventive and like to show off.
- English has lots of dialects and so we get lots of variety.
- Teenagers like to invent their own words so that other people can't understand their 'code'.
- Language changes over time and words are constantly being invented, borrowed and created.
- We like to borrow words from different cultures.

5 Further work

With a partner in class, or as homework, students work on **Worksheet 4.20**, finding as many different words as they can for **friend, a foolish person** and **something that's really good**.

Worksheet 4.20

Suggested answers

Starter activity

Standard: very nice, excellent, good, girl, boy, great, nasty.

Non-standard: sweet*, bangin', sound as a pound, shady*, lass, wicked, bird*, laughin'*, gaffer, yorkie, mint*, girt.

*These words also have a different standard meaning

Activity 1, page 166

Suggested answers are provided on **Worksheet 4.21**.

Further work

Students should find this activity straightforward but here are some suggestions:

Friend – chum, pal, butty, buddy, bestie, comrade, mukkah

A foolish person – fool, numptie, birdbrain, sap, clown, clod, halfwit, nitwit, loon

Worksheet 4.21

Something really good – superb, sound, marvellous, prime, neat, boss, bad, nice, rad, splendid

Controlled assessment guidance
Study of spoken language

Introduction

This section of the Teacher Guide provides you with guidance on the new controlled assessment element of the WJEC specification. It aims to familiarise you with the WJEC Specification requirements for GCSE English Language and GCSE English and help you to teach the controlled assessment tasks in Speaking and listening/ Studying spoken language.

Controlled assessment is compulsory for all students and is not tiered. Specific differentiation advice for Higher and Foundation students is included in this guidance.

Specification requirements

Task-setting

Candidates are required to complete a single controlled assessment unit in the study of spoken language. Each controlled assessment unit may contain more than one task. Tasks must be selected from a number of comparable tasks provided by WJEC. Guidance will be given on the use of source or research material, including access to users of language beyond the classroom. Candidates make a written response. The tasks will be replaced each year.

Task-taking

During the **research and planning** stage, candidates must work under limited supervision. They may work collaboratively in discussion groups and research activities to gather their samples of spoken language, but must provide individual responses which are sufficient to be assessed. Candidates may make use of research materials in the preparation period, and teachers may give advice of a general kind. Detailed writing frames or draft responses to the task should not be used, although some general guidance may be given to help focus the work. Materials used at this stage should be submitted with the final piece of work for assessment and moderation.

Final outcomes must be produced under formal supervision. Where the response takes place over a number of sessions, all candidates' work (including research notes) must be collected and retained securely within the centre between assessment sessions. Extra

time will be allowed to those candidates who qualify for it under existing regulations.

Task-marking

Teachers are expected to mark candidates' work using the assessment criteria provided by WJEC. Work should contain both in-text annotation and a brief summative comment. The Spoken language controlled assessment will be marked out of 20.

The notional relationship between marks and grades is expected to be as follows:

Grade	Mark
U	0–3
G	4–5
F	6–7
E	8–9
D	10–11
C	12–13
B	14–15
A	16–17
A*	19–20

In studying spoken language, learners are expected to:
- reflect and comment critically on their own and others' uses of language in different contexts and discuss how they adapt language to different listeners and tasks, exploring these experiences in the contexts of wider language use and variation
- understand attitudes towards standard and non-standard forms of language and how they vary over time and place
- analyse the characteristics of and influences on spoken language.

Assessment criteria

The assessment criteria for this area of study are:

AO2 Study of spoken language
- Understand variations in spoken language, explaining why language changes in relation to contexts
- Evaluate the impact of spoken language choices in their own and others' use

The controlled assessment assignment will be a sustained response to their own or others' use of spoken language presented by recording, transcript or recollection. 'Controlled' implies that students will attempt their work in examination-type conditions with a strict time limit.

The nature of spoken language in its pure state (speech) is short-lived, so candidates will be allowed during the research and planning stage to gather recordings and to make transcriptions or notes that they can take into the assessment.

Task-taking

During the 8 hours of the teaching and learning stage, students may have access to resources and advice. Transcripts and recordings can be made during this period and teachers may advise students on approaches.

In the final assessment session, students are allowed 2 hours to complete their piece of work. It is not necessary for students to produce the whole piece at the same assessment session, as long as the complete time taken does not exceed 2 hours.

Students are not allowed to take drafts into the final assessment session. Transcripts of spoken language may be word-processed, annotated and highlighted and taken into the controlled assessment.

If the assessment session is divided into shorter periods of time, all the students' work must be collected and stored safely.

Differentiation by task and range

To create tasks suitable for Foundation and for Higher Tier students a number of strategies are possible.

1 Differentiation by task

In the Foundation and Higher Student Books, similar tasks are differentiated by how many speakers the student looks at, for example:

- the Foundation Tier student task can be to look at the language of **one** of the participants, e.g. just the teacher, in the language change task (see Foundation Student Book, pages 160–161).
- the Higher Tier student task can be to look at the language of the teacher **and** of the students in the language change task (see Higher Student Book, pages 158–159).

2 Differentiation by range

Where 1 above is not feasible, such as in the language variation task in the Student Books, then differentiation can be by the amount of material recorded and transcribed (quantity) or by the range of language features and contextual issues discussed by the candidate.

Marking and external moderation

The work will be marked within the centre, using the assessment criteria provided by WJEC. Each piece will be marked out of 20, using the established WJEC mark structure. The assessment criteria for spoken language are set out below. These bands can be related to the 20-mark range and the related grades.

Band 1 (1–3 marks) Candidates show:
- Limited awareness of how spoken language is used
- Limited understanding of factors that influence spoken language
- A little ability to explain obvious differences in language
- A little ability to analyse and evaluate variations and changes in spoken language.

Band 2 (4–7 marks) Candidates show:
- Some awareness of how speakers use spoken language
- Some understanding of the main influences on speakers' language choices
- Limited ability to explain how differences in speech may affect communication
- Limited ability to analyse and evaluate how language changes.

Band 3 (8–11 marks) Candidates show:
- Clear awareness of how spoken language is adapted
- Clear understanding of the different influences on speakers' language choices
- Understanding and begin to explain effects of speech variations
- Some ability to analyse and evaluate how language changes.

Band 4 (12–15 marks) Candidates show:
- Confident awareness of how spoken language is adapted
- Sound understanding of significant influences on speakers' language choices
- Clear explanation of the significance of speech variations
- Clear ability to analyse and evaluate effect of language changes.

Band 5 (16–20 marks) Candidates show:
- Confident awareness of how spoken language is selected and adapted
- Sophisticated understanding of subtle influences on speakers' language choices
- Perceptive explanation of the impact of significant features of speech variations
- Sustained ability to analyse and evaluate susceptibility to variation of features of language changes.

It will be expected that internal moderation will establish a rank order from which the sample will be chosen for the external moderator. All students and teachers will have to sign a coversheet as proof of authenticity. Details of tasks and marks will also be entered on this coversheet, which will accompany students' folders if they are sent to the external moderator.

All centres will receive a brief report on the work of the students and the standard of assessment.

Planning

Practical approaches

As the study of spoken language is new at GCSE, it would be sensible to build up familiarity with spoken language and its attendant ideas over a period of time before the preparation period begins. Students are more than familiar with speech itself and with accent, dialect and slang, so spoken language offers a new area of study with a wealth of material within easy reach.

You may feel nervous as a teacher going into this new area, but the demands for technical vocabulary are few. (A glossary of useful terms is given on Worksheet 4.22.) Teachers should use their own judgement on how much of this vocabulary should be introduced to their students. The intention is not to baffle with jargon but to introduce a handful of useful terms that neatly sum up language features. Teachers may wish to increase their own depth of knowledge over a period of time as their interests develop in what is a fascinating area of study.

An approach to teaching spoken language

- Over a period of time, teach the skills and basic vocabulary for the study of spoken language. These are looked at in more detail on pages 92–97 of this Teacher Guide and link to the relevant pages in the Student Book.
- Allow students an opportunity to practise these skills on samples of speech and on transcripts (see pages 94–5, worksheets 4.5–4.7 and the website for samples).
- Useful ideas, concepts and vocabulary can be fed into teaching at this stage.
- Introduce the chosen tasks for the year and perhaps consider the three approaches – change, choice and variation – though you may wish to limit your students to one of these. At this stage, teachers can best help students by advising against unrealistic and over-complex tasks.
- Students will wish to record, recall and/or transcribe spoken language at this stage. The 8 hours of

preparation time should be sufficient for recording, transcribing or the gathering of relevant material for language variation.
- Teachers are allowed to advise on useful approaches, features to look for in data, simple analytical tools, and the general approach to constructing an answer.
- Arrange a time for the final assessment session. Students are allowed 2 hours in total for the written response and it is the centre's choice as to how this time may be divided. These 2 hours should be considered as 'writing time'. The analysis of language can be carried out in the preparation phase.
- The final assessment session may take place in the classroom or, perhaps more conveniently, in an examination hall where a larger number of students may be tested at once.
- Students should have transcripts and recordings with them (with earphones). They should not have partially written answers or writing frames, though they may annotate or highlight sections of their transcripts illustrating particular features of speech.
- If the assessment session spreads over more than one lesson, ensure that work is securely stored. Students may not redraft work when the assessment session (or sessions) is over.
- Make sure all students have signed a coversheet.
- Keep the work securely in readiness for the submission of the moderation sample.
- Retain the work until 6 months after the examination results are published.
- Students will be able to resubmit their work for one new assessment occasion.
- Since the course is unitised, students may submit a complete controlled assessment folder (including the necessary language study content) at any of the timetabled assessment occasions across the 2- or 1-year course (January and June).

Spoken language

Capturing spoken language

The good news

Spoken language precedes writing in the history of all languages, and we learn to speak fluently before we learn to read and write. Spoken language is all around us and we may speak (and certainly hear) upwards of 10,000 words a day. These words can inform, instruct, amuse, persuade, and tell us that we belong and are valued. We have spoken language at home, at work, on the radio, on television, on record, on film; and as teachers, we speak for a living. Every day we speak and hear a wide range of vocabulary, different grammatical styles, accents, dialect words, slang, taboo language and specialist vocabulary (jargon), so in terms of experience we are all experts in spoken English.

The not quite so good news

Unfortunately for us, spoken English does have the habit of slipping away as soon as we have used it, unless we make special arrangements to store it. This is best done by recording and can also be achieved by turning speech into writing.

Features of speech

If you are new to speech you might be tempted to think of it as a kind of written language produced through sound. In fact, although it is obviously linked to written English, speech does have fundamental differences.

Speech is...	Writing is...
dynamic, interactive, time-bound, informal, spontaneous, face-to-face, social, very sensitive to context, quickly produced and exchanged, personal, and focused on a specific audience	static, impersonal, carefully organised, permanent, compact of expression, space-bound and relatively context-free
Features of speech...	Features of writing...
intonation, volume, rhythm, pause, interruption, overlap, vocal stress, accent	pages, lines, punctuation, capitalisation, error-correction, paragraphs, sentences

Recording speech

Recording speech used to be the sole domain of enthusiasts with reel-to-reel tape recorders. Nowadays a speech-recording function is available on mobile phones, video cameras, PDAs (mobile registers) and laptops, and on special devices like digital voice recorders, which have a built-in USB device that plugs into a computer. Voice files can be sent by email, saved on a memory stick and copied on to CD-ROMs and ipods. If students want to use spontaneous speech from television, they have the advantage of video-recording in all its forms.

Practicalities when recording

- Students may be tempted to push their recording device near the face of a speaker. This will not only annoy the speaker but may also make them self-conscious of their speech to the point where they stop talking. Most built-in microphones adjust to the volume of sound. A little testing beforehand will show students how to get the clearest results.
- Recording one voice is straightforward, two can overlap, three can be messy, and four can be chaotic. With background noise, trains, dogs and mums with

cups of tea, the world can be a noisy place when you want to record. Start with the simplest set-up and see what students can cope with.

Try to avoid scripted speech

Scripted speech starts out as writing, so it remains very much like writing. If your students want to study the speech of *EastEnders* or *Coronation Street*, then they must be made aware of the difference between scripted speech and spontaneous speech. The dialogue on *EastEnders*, for example, is scripted so that overlaps and simultaneous speech are avoided. That makes it quite different from everyday speech where these features are common.

Most scenes in soap operas have a limited number of characters so that overlapping speech can be avoided. This kind of spoken language is simulated rather than authentic, and should be avoided. Normal speech seems much more chaotic than written language and scripted speech, mainly because of the speed with which we speak and also because of the constant gestures, eye contact, and voice qualities we use to add nuance to what we say.

Good choices for your students

Radio phone-ins, chat shows, sports commentary, discussions between students, interviews with participants on game shows, recordings of people going about their everyday conversational lives. The guiding principle is to use spontaneous speech, not rehearsed or scripted speech.

Not-so-good choices

Scripted dialogue, the speech of slick professionals and presenters (unless contrasted with more realistic speech), over-rehearsed speech, edited speech such as news broadcasts, weather forecasts, soap operas, most comedy routines (unfortunately). However, programmes such as *Mock the Week* and *Have I Got News for You* will have a good range of spontaneous speech as well as the scripted material of the presenter.

It would be acceptable and interesting, for example, to investigate speech on *Who Wants to be a Millionaire* or *The Weakest Link*, where the presenter has a formula to follow but the contestant doesn't. Comparison would be a Higher Tier task, whereas the study of one speaker would tend to be a Foundation task.

Other kinds of recording

Students may not always need to record every word. If they are studying dialect words or the latest trendy youth speech, they may be on the lookout for individual words and phrases. These can easily be recorded in writing, in a suitable table, though pronunciation may be lost without recording. Again the 8 hours of preparation are the time to carry out this research. Websites such as the *BBC Voices http://www.bbc.co.uk/voices* site are very useful.

A word about transcribing

Making a transcript from a recording is time-consuming, though it does teach you a lot about spoken language. Rewinding the recording and playing it again and again is the only way to get an accurate written representation that you can work on in a practical way. If you think your students will benefit from taking a transcript into the controlled assessment task, then encourage them to do it. It takes patience, concentration and accuracy – all valuable skills. Don't let them try to transcribe too much, and encourage them to be selective when they choose their sections of speech to transcribe or they will become tired and lose motivation.

What's the point?

The only reason to go to the trouble of making a transcript is to make life easier. You definitely strip the life and colour (accent, intonation, pace, etc.) from speech, but you gain convenience, and it may be easier to see a feature on the page than to hear it. If students make transcripts, they should keep and use the recording for extra information such as accent and the more dynamic aspects of sound.

Practicalities of transcribing

Transcripts can be complex or straightforward, and there is a range of styles but no standard method. Students should keep transcripts as simple as they can, and only transcribe what is going to be useful to them. The table below shows the most useful features and isn't too complex (this table is also available on Worksheet 4.4).

Language change, choice and variation

These are the generic tasks suggested by WJEC. They are used for the sample tasks in the Student Books. Students choose **one** of these approaches.

Language change allows students to study how language changes to meet the needs of the context or situation in which it is produced. In the Student Books it is defined as follows:

'Language **change** is about how language changes to fit different contexts. For example, we don't speak the same way in a playground as we do in a doctor's surgery.'

The worked example in the Student Books uses classroom language. In the guidance section on pages 98–103, examples of other contexts will be given, with further exemplars on the website and in this Teacher Guide.

Language choice enables the study of spoken language from the perspective of the producer of that language. In the Student Books it is defined as follows:

'Candidates explore how their own and others' uses of language is adapted in the contexts of wider language use and variation. The following situations would provide appropriate contexts:
*   responding to older or younger listeners
*   responding to people in authority
*   talking to peers and family
*   responding to strangers.'

The worked example in the Student Books shows an example of responding to people in authority. In the guidance section below, examples of other language choices will be given with further exemplars on the website.

Symbol	What it means	What it tells us
(.)	Pause	Usually less than half a second long. We use them in our speech to punctuate what we say and to give ourselves time to think, e.g. Oh (.) right (.) ok then (.)
(2)	Pause in seconds	Check the longer pauses. Usually they mean something is going on, such as waiting for a reply or thinking
Underlined word(s)	Emphasis	Have a close look at why these words have been given extra emphasis
(coughs)	Other noises	Other contextual details
( )	Unidentifiable speech	Used when you really can't make out what was said
T, S	Initial of speaker	For example, T for teacher, S for student
Um, er, uh	Hesitation noises	These sounds should be recorded as they show us that the speaker is uncertain or hesitant for some reason

Language variation enables the study of language variation across a wider perspective of language styles. In the Student Books it is defined as follows:

'Candidates demonstrate their understanding of the reasons for and effects of these choices, and how they may vary over time and place. The following situations would provide appropriate contexts:

- using non-standard forms to peers and family
- using standard forms to strangers and those in authority
- the effects of standard and non-standard forms in television and radio advertising.'

The worked example in the Student Books shows variation in a school context, though there is a wide range of contexts available. Television and radio offer a wide range of opportunities to study accent in particular, though it is important to ensure that any material gathered is primarily unscripted and spontaneous. Language variation is mostly a matter of vocabulary. It focuses on a range of dialect and slang terms that always begin in speech. Script writers will use dialect, accent, slang terms and non-standard verbs to give their scripts and soap operas authenticity. This means that scripted material sometimes can be useful for sourcing the way spoken language varies as it does reflect real usage, in some respects - vocabulary, some non-standard verb forms, but it can never be taken as a facsimile of genuine spontaneous speech. It's too organised, too controlled, and doesn't reflect the way we trim and shape and correct what we are saying even as we say it. Examples of suitable material are given in the guidance section below.

Spoken language – what your students need to do

Start with an area of spoken language that students are interested in, and then use the principle of best fit when deciding whether to use change, choice or variation. Teachers can advise here on the most useful category.

The intention is to offer students (and teachers) a flexible approach that will help them choose a controlled assessment task to suit their interests.

Language change – sample controlled assessment activities

Any context or situation develops its own language rules and vocabulary over time. Take for example the short transcript below.

Waitress: Hello. Are you ready to order?

Customer: Yes. We'd like one scampi and chips and a rump steak with salad.
Waitress: How would you like the steak done?
Customer: Medium rare please.
Waitress: Anything to drink?
Customer: Yes, a coke and a glass of white wine.
Waitress: Thank you.

Areas of interest here

There is a specific vocabulary for this situation and a formula that is familiar but rarely the same every time. The question/answer structure, politeness features, shared understanding and specific vocabulary are the main areas of interest. While this is unlikely to be enough for a controlled assessment, three transcripts of this length for similar exchanges, or one lengthier exchange, would give enough material.

Differentiation between Higher and Foundation

Differentiation can be managed through the task (Foundation – 'How does the waitress change her language to suit the situation?' Higher – 'How do the waitress **and** the customer change their language to suit the situation?')

Or through the number of transcripts made (i.e. two or three service situations)

Or through the length of transcript (i.e. one service situation but include ordering, delivery and payment).

Suggested tasks for language change

- **In the workplace** – as experienced perhaps on work placement **or** experience of everyday workplaces – cafes, supermarket checkouts, shops.
- **On television** – sporting commentary, live discussion, unscripted speech from music programmes (band interviews), guest interviews (Jools Holland, Jonathan Ross, Jeremy Kyle, etc.), including resources on BBC iplayer, YouTube, etc.
- **In the classroom** – with permission!
- **Problem-solving** – giving directions, explaining a procedure, making decisions. These can be organised in class, e.g. the balloon game, desert survival, role-playing games **or** through resources such as YouTube and VideoJug, where there are many instructional videos created by amateurs.

Language choice – sample controlled assessment activities

1 With any given audience we choose our language to suit the listener. In the Student Books the theme taken up was responding to people in authority. Here is an example using the 'responding to older or younger listeners' idea. The child is 3 years and 3 months old, and is discussing the story 'Goldilocks and the Three Bears' with her mother before bed.

Mother: How does it start with the story?
Child: and then she went in the woods
Mother: In the <u>woods</u>?
Child: And she saw a house (.)
Mother: Yeah
Child: And she (.) and she opened the door and she said (.)
Mother: Yeah
Child: <u>Hello</u> (.) <u>helloo</u>
Mother: Yeah
Child: And she saw a porridge (.) and she tried the daddy bear's (.) and she ate (.) and it was <u>too hot</u>|
Mother: <u>Right</u>|
Child: So she tasted the mummy bear's but it was too <u>cold</u>|
Mother: yeah|
Child: And she tried the baby bear's and it was just right
Mother: Oh, so what did she do?
Child: She ate it all up (.) um
Mother: oh oh (.) piggy Goldilocks (.) what happened then?

The mother's language choices are closely linked to her purpose here. They seem to cover a range of purposes – to entertain, to educate, to complete the ritual of a story before sleep, and to maintain the close bond between them.

Areas of interest
- The mother's frequent questions to start and to continue the conversation
- Her minimal responses (frequent use of 'yeah' and 'right') to give immediate feedback, to maintain turn-taking
- Her playful and dramatic joining in with the story-telling process 'oh, oh, piggy Goldilocks'
- The mother's exaggerated intonation mirrored in the child's story-telling mode, e.g. mother and child both use emphasis on particular words
- Her simplified vocabulary and her use of simple grammatical structures

- Foundation could look at just the mother's speech, or just the child's. Higher could look at both.
- At both levels, students could use two or three short transcripts to illustrate different features.

Suggested tasks for language choice
- **Responding to older or younger listeners** – talking to younger siblings, this can be the student themselves or how a parent or parents do this. Similarly, interaction with someone from the grandparents' generation, studying one or both speakers depending on level.
- **Responding to people in authority** – as the example in the Student Books, although any authority figure would work, depending on permission and confidentiality.
- **Talking to peers and family** – as in the Student Books, but this also opens up the range of peer-group language as well as 'family' words – both as 'badges of membership'.
- **Responding to strangers** – this could be a careers interview, an interview with an employer for work experience, a school visitor, etc. The key idea is that the language choices are affected by the speaker not being familiar with the person they are addressing.

Language variation – sample controlled assessment activities

Language variation focuses in on standard and non-standard forms, particularly accent, dialect and slang. The WJEC specification outlines the following areas:
- using non-standard forms to peers and family
- using standard forms to strangers and those in authority
- the effects of standard and non-standard forms in television and radio advertising.

Language variation within the family can be both generational and geographic. This transcript from the BBC television programme *Word on the Street* illustrates the possibilities very well. The BBC footage of this clip can be found on ActiveTeach (**Video clip 4.1**).

(At a family barbecue)
BBC Voices (Nick Hancock) – Leicester family Grandma Doreen, Grandson James, Auntie Sarah, Jane

NH: Meet three generations of a Leicestershire family (4) they all speak the same language (.) but they've all got their own way with words (2) Grandma Doreen knows some wonderfully expressive old words.

Doreen: she was mardy (1) she was miserable (.) she was sulky

NH: Grandson James uses some rather unfamiliar new ones

James: Like you're walking down the street and he goes like that girl (.) bison

James' friend: bison

NH: Auntie Sarah is proud of her local accent

Auntie Sarah: (strong Leicester accent) I'm working class girl (.) I don't come from an office it's obvious by the way I talk I would have said

NH: Her sister Jane has spent most of her life changing one accent for another

Jane: (RP accent) I've been working in the sort of environment where a (.) regional accents aren't used so I've gradually (.) dropped mine (5)
(background noise)

NH: The sisters' voices and those of their family and friends all tell a story (.) it's the story of why we talk to each other in Britain today the way we do
[4.14]

Sarah: Well I would say I talk totally different to my elder sister Jane … purely cause of the way our lives have gone

Jane: I mean I think the sort of boys I used to go for were different to the sorts of boys [you went for] [yes]

Sarah: [Like you used to hang out] with all the boffs at school and I just hung out with the naughty people

Jane: we didn't have boffs then

Sarah: yes you did

Other voice: yes you did

Other voice: yes you did
[4:57]

Family member: Jane talks more educated I would say (2) to be polite (laughs)

Jane: bit more proper like

Sister: She's a librarian, what more can you say (laughs)

Family member: How do librarians speak

Other voice: like Jane

Sister: well she (.) she puts it on

Brother in law: she's posh (laughs) Sarah's (.) Sarah's as common as muck (.) I associate more with Sarah than Jane
(family groans)

Areas of interest

This transcript illustrates very well a range of variation tied to age, social class and geography. Students could study how language varies according to the age of the family member (Grandma Doreen or Grandson James in the example above) **or** social class (the differences in speech between Aunt Sarah and Jane) **or** by geography (variations in accent between different areas of a city or county).

Differentiation between Higher and Foundation

Differentiation can be managed through the task (Foundation – 'How does Barack Obama change his language to meet the needs of his audience?' Higher – 'How does Barack Obama change his language to meet the needs of his audience and his own need to win the election?')

Or through the number of transcripts made (i.e. two or three brief transcripts)

Or through the length of transcript (i.e. one speech covering formal and informal styles).

Suggested tasks for language variation (standard and non-standard forms)

1   Record and transcribe or discuss and make notes on the speech of your local area. You might want to record a group discussion amongst your friends or family or classmates. What special 'local' words do you use? What do you think of your accent when you hear it on TV or radio? What do people from other areas think of it?

2   How are different accents and dialects used on television or radio? You could look at (or listen to) adverts for different products. Which ones use standard English and an RP accent? Which products use a West Country or Scottish accent? Record and transcribe some examples for your notes. Do certain products use a certain accent? What is the connection between the product being sold and the accent being used?

Useful questions to ask of any spoken text

(Try them out on the sample transcripts)

1   Who are the participants in the conversation?

2   What are their roles?

3   What is the purpose of the exchange?

4   How is the speech affected by the context or situation it takes place in?

5   Is the manner of the conversation formal or informal?

6   Is the grammar standard or non-standard?

7   What is the topic of the conversation?

8   Who controls the topic?

Controlled assessment guidance
Literary reading

Introduction

This section of the Teacher Guide provides you with guidance on the new controlled assessment element of the WJEC specification. It aims to familiarise you with the WJEC specification requirements for GCSE English, GCSE English Language or GCSE English Literature and help you to teach the controlled assessment tasks in Literary reading.

Controlled assessment is compulsory for all students and is not tiered. Specific differentiation advice for Higher and Foundation students is included in this guidance. Student example answers are included to demonstrate successful answers to help you become familiar with the controlled assessment marking criteria.

Course requirements

GCSE English
Shakespeare and Literary Heritage Poetry
Different Cultures prose

GCSE English Language
Extended Literary text

GCSE English Literature
Linked texts: Shakespeare and Literary Heritage Poetry

Guidance

Specification requirements

GCSE English and GCSE English Language Assessment Objectives

The Assessment Objectives for GCSE English and GCSE English Language are identical. QCDA requires the Assessment Objectives to be covered by the entire assessment structure, but it is the choice of the awarding body where each Assessment Objective is tested. Hence the first and third bullet points of AO2 will be assessed principally in the externally assessed Unit 1.

AO2
- Read and understand texts, selecting material appropriate to purpose, collating from different sources and making comparisons and cross-references as appropriate
- Develop and sustain interpretations of writers' ideas and perspectives

- Explain and evaluate how writers use linguistic, grammatical, structural and presentational features to achieve effects and engage and influence the reader.
- Understand texts in their social, cultural and historical context

GCSE English Literature Assessment Objectives

Not all the GCSE English Literature Assessment Objectives are being tested in the controlled assessment unit. For example, AO3 states that students must 'make comparisons', but this aspect is tested in Unit 1 and is only peripheral to the controlled assessment unit where 'explaining links' is more central. It will be noticed that AO4, which is concerned with 'social, cultural and historical contexts' does not appear in the controlled assessment unit, since this is covered in the external assessment units.

AO1: Respond to texts critically and imaginatively; select and evaluate relevant textual detail to illustrate and support interpretations.

AO2: Explain how language, structure and form contribute to writers' presentation of ideas, themes and settings.

AO3: Make comparisons and explain links between texts, evaluating writers' different ways of expressing meaning and achieving effects.

Task-setting

WJEC will set generic tasks for all the reading assignments, with example tasks based on particular texts. The generic tasks give teachers basic guidance on the type of assignment appropriate and the particular focus. Centres can devise a similar task suited to their students. All generic and exemplar tasks will be available on the secure WJEC website in the April preceding the beginning of the two year course. In preparation for the tasks, it is expected that the texts will be taught and then the task introduced so that the approaches may be discussed in the classroom. At this stage, students may make notes and teachers may comment on their work. For the Shakespeare/Poetry linked task (GCSE English and GCSE English Literature), a selection of the WJEC Poetry Collection will be specified each year, and students are expected to have studied at least ten of the poems specified.

Task preparation

Shakespeare and Literary Heritage Poetry (GCSE English and English Literature)

Teachers must choose a suitable Shakespeare play and a selection of the poems from those specified by WJEC. After the play and poems have been studied in class, students may start to think about possible responses to the task set by their teacher. As noted above, the teacher can adapt a sample task or create a new one, but it must be one that enables students to fulfil the Assessment Objectives. In their preparatory work, students may make notes and work with other students. They are not allowed to write drafts. It is suggested that students plan their essay in three parts: a consideration of the thematic aspect in relation to the Shakespeare play; a consideration of the thematic aspect in relation to the poems; a section where the two texts are linked.

Different Cultures prose (GCSE English)

After studying a Different Cultures prose text from the GCSE English Literature set text list, students should be given a task based on the generic task provided by WJEC. Again, in their preparation for the actual task, students may make notes and plan out their work.

Extended Literary text (GCSE English Language)

For this task, teachers may choose any Shakespeare play or a prose or drama text from the GCSE English Literature set text list. The generic task set will be based on character or the way the writer creates atmosphere; thus it will be different from the thematically based GCSE English and GCSE English Literature Shakespeare/Poetry linked task. Again, sample tasks will be set and centres may adapt the sample task to suit their students.

Task-taking

The final assessment session will take place at some time convenient for the centre. For all the tasks except the linked Shakespeare and Literary Heritage poetry, students will be given up to 2 hours to complete their work. The Shakespeare/Poetry assignment will have a time allowance of 4 hours, since two texts have to be considered. As with the Writing tasks, the assessment time may be divided up. If the assessment session is divided into shorter periods of time, all the students' work must be collected and stored safely between the assessment sessions. Once the work is complete, it may not be revised or resubmitted. Candidates may have clean copies of the WJEC Poetry Collection and the texts during the assessment sessions. Whether or not students had access to clean copies of the texts during

the assessment period must be noted on the controlled assessment coversheet. Students may also have one sheet of notes in the assessment session. These notes may not contain a draft or plan, and the sheet must be included with the student's folder, if it is chosen for the moderation sample. It is important that these notes, therefore, are kept with the work when it is collected for assessment. Students may word-process their responses, but they must not have access to the internet or to their personal school computer files, and for their GCSE English and GCSE English Language work they may not have access to dictionaries or spell-checker/grammar programs.

All students must sign coversheets to authenticate their work.

Marking and external moderation

When the work is complete, it should be marked in the usual way, using the assessment criteria. Students may be told their marks, but are not allowed to revise their work. The work will be assessed within the centre and internally cross-moderated to establish a reliable rank order and to ensure parity of standards. An external moderator will be appointed by the Board.

All students and teachers will have to sign a coversheet as proof of authenticity. Details of tasks and marks will also be entered on this coversheet, which will accompany students' folders if they are sent to the external moderator.

All centres will receive a brief report on the work of the students and the standard of assessment.

The maximum number of marks for each controlled assessment Reading assignment will be as follows:

GCSE English

Shakespeare/Poetry essay	20 marks
Different Cultures prose essay	20 marks

GCSE English Language

Extended Literary text essay	40 marks

GCSE English Literature

Shakespeare/Poetry essay	40 marks

In the GCSE English folder the work on Shakespeare and Poetry is worth 10% of the total mark and will be marked out of 20, while in GCSE English Literature it is worth 25% of the total mark and will be marked out of 40.

The WJEC Poetry Collection

The WJEC Poetry Collection will be free for all centres taking the examinations. The Collection comprises English, Welsh and Irish Literary Heritage verse; it is thematically arranged and contains poems ranging from the testing to the relatively straightforward. For each assessment year, WJEC will specify two thematically grouped lists of poems, and it is expected that students will study at least ten of these. Study of these poems will support students' preparation for the Unit 1 external assessment, as well as being the basis for choice in the linked Shakespeare/Poetry assignment. The selected poems will be on the WJEC website from the April of the year preceding the beginning of the Key Stage 4 teaching and will be grouped in the following themes:

- Love
- Family and parent/child relationships
- Youth/age
- Power and ambition
- Male/female relationships and the role of women
- Hypocrisy/prejudice
- Conflict
- Grief.

Since a number of poems in the Collection could fit into a number of thematic areas, WJEC will specify a variety of verse which could be used in various contexts.

Tasks and texts

As noted above, most controlled assessment Reading and Literature tasks must be based on texts in the GCSE English Literature set text lists which can be found in the current specifications. The only exceptions to this requirement are that:

- for the GCSE English linked Shakespeare/Poetry assignment, any Shakespeare text may be chosen
- for the GCSE English Literature linked Shakespeare/ Poetry assignment, any Shakespeare play may be chosen except the two in the GCSE English Literature set text list
- for the GCSE English Language Extended Literacy text task, any Shakespeare play may be chosen in addition to those on the GCSE English Literature set text list.

Linked Shakespeare and Literary Heritage Task (common to GCSE English and GCSE English Literature)

The reason for making this a common task across the two specifications is that there are likely to be students who embark on a double GCSE course and, finding it too demanding, switch to GCSE English instead. The work they may have completed for their English Literature folder can be used in their English folder and there will be no need for them to repeat this work, though as noted above, the total mark will be different for the two specifications.

The thematic task will be structured in three parts. The first will focus on the Shakespeare play, taking the generic task as the basis. The second will be based on

poems from the Collection. Here the focus is likely to be on one poem, though students should refer to others in their writing. In the final part of the task, students will be expected to make links between the texts.

GCSE English Literature Assessment Objective AO3 requires students to 'Make comparisons and explain links between texts, evaluating writers' different ways of expressing meaning and achieving effects.' The comparative aspect is covered in Unit 1 of the GCSE English Literature examination, so in the controlled assessment it will only be necessary for students to show how the two texts take different attitudes to a common theme. They may wish to include some comparative aspects, though this is not a requirement.

Extracts from a linked Shakespeare/Poetry essay

The student whose work is quoted below had studied *Macbeth* and a group of poems concerned with responses to learning about the death of a loved one. The essay focuses on Act 4 scene 3 of the play and on Donne's sonnet 'Since she whom I lov'd'. The essay title was:

When Macduff hears of the death of his wife and children in Act 4 scene 3, he expresses his grief. Within the context of the whole play, consider his reaction to death in relation to John Donne's reaction to the death of his wife in the sonnet 'Since she whom I lov'd'. In your answer refer to other poems relating to this theme.

The student begins with a consideration of the poem.

In this sonnet, John Donne talks about the loss of his wife. Like Ben Jonson in his poem 'On my First Son', he thinks that his loved one is in heaven. However, he worries that his love of his wife will overtake his love of God. Donne sees this as giving in to the world of flesh, in other words to the devil.

He has begun, sensibly, with the thematic aspect noted in the title and then goes on to look at the poem in more detail. He has also referred to another poem in the Collection, suggesting wider reading. He always keeps the 'reaction to death' in the forefront of his thinking. For example, he later writes:

The end of the second line reads: 'so streams do show their heads'. John Donne in this line shows his frustration being afraid of loving his wife more than God. He is suggesting that God is the head of the stream and that everyone will flow towards Him as the 'head' is the main part of anything. This is a paradox since Donne is in danger of loving the stream, which is his wife, more than the head of the stream which is God. Donne uses an extended metaphor comparing both God and his wife to water. He comments that God quenches his thirst and he feels that he should be satisfied with that. However, the next line begins with 'But' suggesting that he is doubting himself.

The student goes on to analyse the remainder of the poem, finishing with:

In the final couplet, he again speaks to God as a friend and reassures Him that he will not become committed to the 'world, flesh, yea devil'. The sonnet shows his deep affection for his lost wife and links that love to his relationship with God.

Having considered the poem, the student moves on to the drama.

In the play, Macbeth is terrified that Macduff, now he has fled to England, will try to lead a rebellion against him. He decides to slaughter the rest of his family, not realising that this will make Macduff even more angry. In the scene Act 4 scene 2, we witness the horrific murder of Lady Macduff and her children. The news of these deaths is taken to Macduff in London, where he is speaking with Malcolm.

The student has put the scene into context and shown an understanding and knowledge of the rest of the play, which is a requirement of the specification. He then moves on to the scene where Ross tells Macduff of Macbeth's murder of his family:

The first thing that happens in the scene is that Macduff asks Ross 'How does my wife?' This suggests that he is a family man and concerned about his wife and children. Ross hesitates in his reply both to this question and the one which follows about the health of his children. Ross knows that Macbeth has murdered both wife and children, but does not know how to break it to Macduff. His reply 'Why well' is ambiguous and Macduff interprets it as meaning that they are indeed 'well'. We know that Ross really means that they are safe in heaven.

The student continues by analysing the next part of the scene leading up to the revelation:

'Your castle is surpris'd, your wife and babes savagely slaughtered'. Macduff's grief is emphasised by his constant return to the information, questioning Ross, 'My wife killed too?' … 'All my pretty ones?' His feelings for his children here reflect Ben Jonson's sadness over the death of his son. Malcolm says 'Merciful heaven', making a religious reference in a similar way to Donne, and tells Macduff to 'give sorrow words'. His next line is 'The grief that does not speak/Whispers the o'er-fraught heart and bids it break'. In a way this line sums up all the poetry I have read relating to mourning a death, as the poems are all about relieving the grief through talking or writing.

He goes on to look at the way in which the scene develops and the methods by which Ross and Malcolm help Macduff to come to terms with his loss, turning his energies and emotions to thoughts of revenge. The student ends with the 'linking' aspect, which is likely to be rather shorter than the two analytic parts that preceded it.

In conclusion, the two writers Shakespeare and Donne write differently about the way grief affects people. John Donne's poem is written from personal experience of the loss of someone very dear to him – his wife. He bases his poem on religious ideas and links his love of his wife to his love of God. The poem is deeply religious in both content and imagery. On the other hand Shakespeare in 'Macbeth' talks about grief in a different way. There is no doubt that Macduff feels as deeply as Donne, but his grief is seen in a private meeting with others and he is influenced by their reactions to the situation as well as his own. Donne's grief is highly personal but Macduff's is public. Another link between the two pieces of literature is that they both talk of 'heaven'. Macduff says despairingly, 'Did heaven look on and would not take their part?' meaning that such a terrible deed should have been stopped by heaven. He is angry with God that He let it happen. Donne, though, is much less concerned with that kind of feeling. Donne's poem ends with a resolution that he will try to love God more, but Macduff's situation is open ended since he is going to take revenge for the death of his family. He has been encouraged to turn his grief into anger and bloodlust.

The student clearly makes links between the two pieces of literature in this conclusion and also to some extent compares, which as suggested above is almost inevitable.

Success will come for students who have:
- a good grasp of the Shakespeare play – particularly the scene on which the work will focus
- a clear understanding of the poem chosen for particular consideration
- the ability to write about aspects of the play outside the chosen scene
- the ability to refer to other poems with related themes
- a good understanding of the way the two pieces of literature are thematically linked
- an ability to draw the thematically linked aspects of the literature together and make clear connections between them.

If a student expects high marks, it is essential that they cover the third and fourth bullet points in their response. It is not sufficient to simply write about one scene and one poem, as this would not fulfil the QCDA's requirement that students study a whole play and a group of poems.

In the GCSE English folder, this work will be assessed using the first two parts of AO2:

- Read and understand texts, selecting material appropriate to purpose, collating from different sources and making comparisons and cross-references as appropriate
- Develop and sustain interpretations of writer's ideas and perspectives

In the GCSE English Literature folder, the essay will be assessed using all the Assessment Objectives:

AO1: Respond to texts critically and imaginatively; select and evaluate relevant textual detail to illustrate and support interpretations

AO2: Explain how language, structure and form contribute to writers' presentation of ideas, themes and settings

AO3: Make comparisons and make links between texts; explain how texts have been influential and significant to self and other readers in different contexts and at different times

Although these Assessment Objectives are subtly different in their wording, the main thrust of the assessment will be concerned with students' ability to analyse the way a writer conveys the experience, with a clear emphasis on the stylistic elements.

GCSE English: Different Cultures prose assignment

Students must study a Different Cultures prose text from the GCSE English Literature set text list. Since they have to study a Different Cultures prose text for English Literature, it will be possible for them to fulfil this GCSE English controlled assessment requirement by basing work on a text that they may have originally been preparing for the GCSE English Literature examination. It is likely that the set text list will change as the specification runs its course. Full details may be found in the current specification on the WJEC website.

In this part of the controlled assessment folder, the two Assessment Objectives noted for GCSE English above will be joined by the third column which refers to 'Understanding texts in their social, cultural and historical contexts'. Tasks, therefore, in this section of the folder must reflect these aspects. However, it will not be necessary for students to fill their essays with socio-cultural background. The main thrust of the work must still be on the way that language has been used to create effect.

As with other parts of the folder, a generic task will be provided and centres are free to create their own tasks based on the suggested structure.

Extracts from a Different Cultures prose essay

This student had read and studied Steinbeck's *Of Mice and Men*. She was given the title:

In a letter, Steinbeck wrote of Curley's wife: 'She's a nice girl and not a floozy.' Discuss and explain your own impression of Curley's wife, giving some consideration to the social context she finds herself in.

The task allows students to look at the whole text, and includes some consideration of the socio-cultural aspects. As in any essay on a text, the moderator will be looking for close attention to the language and carefully considered views.

The student begins her essay:

Steinbeck presents Curley's wife as a very complex and emotional character who lives in a world of men. This situation necessarily affects the way she behaves and is seen by both the reader and the men on the ranch. Clearly she feels isolated and lacking in feminine company. The fact that her marriage to Curley does not appear to be either happy or satisfying makes her life seem empty. She fills it with dangerous conversations with the men on the ranch and it is this activity which eventually leads to her tragic death.

In the opening, the student has presented the character in her situation and suggested her generally sympathetic view of the woman. However, the points made so far are assertions and she needs now to back them up with a systematic investigation of Curley's wife's part in the novel. She continues:

Her first appearance in the book occurs when Lennie and George have settled into the bunkhouse. She appears leaning in a provocative way against the doorframe. 'She put her hands behind her chest and leaned forward against the doorframe so that her body was thrown forward.' We also learn that: 'She had full, rouged lips and wide spaced eyes, heavily made up.' Steinbeck adds that 'her fingernails were red' and this colour, which can symbolise passion, is reflected in her 'little bouquets of red ostrich feathers' on her mules. This would seem to suggest a rather flirty character, as she seems to be both dressed and behaving provocatively. However, these details could imply that she enjoys dressing and acting in a feminine way. Also she is young and probably naïve and may not be aware of the effect she is having on the men who watch her. I believe that this description is just a reflection of the outside perception of Curley's wife. It does not necessarily display her true character or how she may have felt inside her heart or soul.

In this section of the essay, the student is 'developing and sustaining' her 'interpretations of the writer's ideas and perspectives'. The references to the text are used to support her views. She is also 'selecting material appropriate to purpose'. She continues:

The men's perception of her is clear. George says to Lennie: 'Don't even take a look at that bitch. I seen 'em poison before, but I never seen no piece of jail bait worse than her.' He goes on to say 'Jesus, what a tramp.' I think Steinbeck does not want the reader to accept these comments as the truth about Curley's wife. They came from a man who has to control Lennie's behaviour very closely and this must colour the way he thinks about her. A little later Curley's wife makes the comment 'I never get to talk to anyone. I get awful lonely'. This makes the reader sympathetic to her and suggests that George's reaction is judgemental and prejudiced.

Again the student displays the ability to probe the text and see that the surface meaning is not necessarily the one that the writer wishes us to take away. A little later in the essay she picks up her point about the prejudice she notices in George's views:

The language used about Curley's wife is violent, dismissive or derogatory: 'Tart', 'heavily made up' and 'bitch' all seem to reflect the view of some men that any woman who was not absolutely perfect in her behaviour and modestly dressed must be a 'tart'. Perhaps the all-male society of the ranch makes the men think in this prejudiced and angry way. The Wall Street Crash led to the Depression in America in the 1930s which resulted in the poverty and lack of hope seen in the wandering ranch hands in the novel. This situation must have made the men angry and lacking in self esteem. Curley's wife becomes a target for all their built-in repressions and frustrations.

Here the student makes clear that she has grasped the social, cultural and historical context. However, she has not simply written an account of the history of the USA in the period, but instead has sensibly linked her historical information to her interpretation of the text and made it relevant to her task.

Later in the essay she looks at Curley's wife's attitude to Crooks, the black worker:

Her attitude towards Crooks is unacceptable and unthinkable. It is demeaning and uncalled for when she says: 'a nigger and a dum dum.' Later in the novel she tells him: 'I could get you strung up on a tree so easy it ain't even funny'. This mean, sinister and cruel attitude was the norm for the time. Again she simply reflects the feelings of her society, though this is not an excuse for the racist view she has. Perhaps she deliberately uses these provocative remarks in order to show her

feminine control, power and authority. She does not have much else to control in the male-dominated world she lives in. The hierarchy of the period puts her below white men but above black men, and she has an opportunity to show her position in the way she treats Crooks. Nevertheless, modern readers do find her treatment of him objectionable and this is a negative side to her character.

Again there is some probing of the text here with a thoughtful investigation of what readers would find unpleasant about the woman. The historical context is again investigated.

The student goes on to look at Curley's wife's frustrated dreams of becoming a film star and her death at the hands of Lennie. The mainly sympathetic assessment of the character ends:

Lastly, I feel that Curley's wife is not a particularly complicated or complex character; she has a simple and naïve mind that most young girls have. It was her surroundings and her frustrated dreams that made her life so hard. Steinbeck deliberately does not give her a name in order to make a statement to show that women at the time did not have independence. Instead they were owned by their husbands. So she does not have an identity or status as a result of society's views about the position of women. Steinbeck created the persona to make people think about the problems 'Curley's wife' and women as a whole faced at the time. She is a tragic figure and deserves our sympathy rather than our disdain.

The essay in its complete form is deeply rooted in text, has a clear idea of the social context and is well structured. The student follows her arguments through and does not baulk at the less pleasant aspects of the woman.

To be successful in this section of the controlled assessment, students need to:
- have a firm and secure understanding of the text
- be able to focus clearly on the task
- plan carefully
- be able to refer to the text with confidence and analyse the references
- be able to include references to the social, cultural and historical contexts when they are relevant to an understanding of the texts.

GCSE English Language: Study of an Extended Literary text

Students may choose any Shakespeare play or a prose or drama text from the GCSE English Literature set-text list for this section of their folder. The generic tasks will be provided by WJEC and, as with other controlled assessment tasks, centres are at liberty to adapt the generic task to suit their students.

The task for this controlled assessment work must be clearly different from that submitted for the English Literature Shakespeare/Poetry linked task. Since the latter is thematic in structure, it is likely that the GCSE English Language extended text work will be based on character analysis or the creation of atmosphere and setting.

The Assessment Objectives for this section of the controlled assessment are:
- Read and understand texts, selecting material appropriate for purpose, collating from different sources and making comparisons and cross-references as appropriate
- Develop and sustain interpretations of writer's ideas and perspectives

As noted above, the aspect of the AO1 concerning 'making comparisons and cross-referencing' is covered principally in Unit 1 of the external assessment.

Extracts from a study of an extended text

This student had studied Shakespeare's *Romeo and Juliet*. She had been given the title:

'"Tybalt and Mercutio represent very different attitudes and approaches to life." How far do you agree with this statement? In your answer, make close reference to the text to support your views.'

This task allows the student to demonstrate her ability to show that she has 'read and understood a text' and to interpret and develop her responses. The task demands that she look at a large part of the play, but gives sufficient focus for her to write about certain aspects of it in detail. While in this controlled assessment task it is important that students display knowledge of the whole text, there is the understanding that in the restricted time allowed, they are well advised to concentrate on an aspect of the text. As noted above, this is likely to be centred on a particular character or characters.

The student begins her essay with a general opening statement in which she places the two men as central to our understanding of the play as a whole:
Throughout Shakespeare's play 'Romeo and Juliet', the themes of love and hate are a strong feature. These themes are displayed in several ways, most importantly in the feud between the Montagues and Capulets. Tybalt acts as a representative of the Capulet family, while Mercutio, a kinsman of the Prince and friend of Romeo, favours the Montague cause. Both men are pivotal characters in the play.

In the opening paragraph the student has established the basic thematic structure of the play and pointed the reader towards her main concern: a consideration of the two chosen characters. In controlled assessment, it is important that students move into the main body of the essay quickly: there is not room or time for extended introductions. She continues by looking at Tybalt in the first scene, carefully building a character based on the text:
Within the first scene of the play Shakespeare immediately represents Tybalt as a fighter through the imperative 'look upon thy death'. This threat to his opponent – Benvolio – gives the impression that he is violent. Shakespeare juxtaposes Benvolio with Tybalt with the line 'I do but keep the peace' suggesting his peacemaking characteristic in stark contrast to Tybalt's desire for blood. Tybalt sees himself as the personification of the feud and is determined to maintain its momentum 'I hate hell, all Montagues and thee'. Since there is no clear and obvious reason for the feud, we see this hatred as unnatural and obsessive. His loyalty to his family, which could be regarded as honourable, is really an excuse to attack and hurt the Montagues, or more probably simply to fight.

In this section of the essay, the student shows by close reference to the text that Tybalt is more interested in violence than restrained and sensible action. She goes on to look at Tybalt's behaviour in the masked ball scene:
During the masked ball scene, Tybalt shows his hatred and his aggressive character. 'What dares the slave', he says when he sees Romeo. The term 'slave' suggests that Tybalt is insulting Romeo and implies that Romeo is weak in comparison with himself. His comment, 'To strike him dead I hold it not a sin' reinforces our view that he is without morals, since he has no real justification for such an action. Ironically, he is over-confident and arrogant in his belief that he could easily kill Romeo, since later in the play Romeo kills him. After Capulet has forcibly stopped Tybalt attacking Romeo during the course of the masked ball, he swears vengeance at a later date for Romeo's intrusion. 'This intrusion shall/ now seeming sweet, convert to bitt'rest gall.' The idea of revenge is often associated with villainous characters and the term 'bitt'rest gall' suggests a mind which is bent on cruelty.

Having established to some extent the unpleasant nature of Tybalt, the student now looks at the development of the character of Mercutio:
The character of Mercutio is introduced in Act 1 scene 4. When he is talking to Romeo, he makes light-hearted fun of his status as a lover. Romeo claims he has a 'soul of lead' to which Mercutio replies 'You are a lover; borrow Cupid's wings/ And soar with them above the common bound'. This

witty response suggests that he has a real interest in Romeo's recovery from Rosaline's rejection of him. This is a caring characteristic and contrasts vividly with Tybalt's desire for revenge. We have some sympathy for Mercutio's sharp dismissal of the romantic love Romeo seems to be suffering from. 'If love be rough with you, be rough with love.' Later, his beautiful and poetic Queen Mab speech marks him out as a sensitive person, however, and his talk of dreams and 'vain fantasy' is markedly different from Tybalt's harsh and unpleasant use of language.

In this section the student makes a clear distinction between the two men's use of language, although for the highest grades there could be more close analysis. In the section that follows this extract, she goes on to look at the way Mercutio dismisses the idea of emotional love. Later in the essay, she turns to the fateful meeting of Tybalt and Mercutio in Act 3 scene 1:

The scene in which Tybalt and Mercutio duel provides much evidence about the two men's attitudes. After Benvolio unsuccessfully tries to persuade Mercutio to 'retire', Mercutio's rather flippant attitude is revealed when Tybalt appears. 'By my heel I care not'. The use of the word 'heel' shows he is mocking and also conveys that he sees the Capulets as inferior. He is not intimidated by the prospect of a fight with them. In this way the two men are rather similar. Both are happy to fight, but Tybalt is determined for revenge while Mercutio looks on the occasion in a less serious way. Tybalt is relatively polite in his first statement: 'Gentlemen, good den: a word with one of you'. Mercutio immediately and sarcastically replies: 'And but one word with one of us? Couple it with something; make it a word and a blow.' It is clear that Tybalt's desire for revenge on Romeo makes him reluctant to waste his time with Mercutio. This only makes Mercutio more determined to fight: 'Here's my fiddlestick; here's that shall make you dance.'

Tybalt is hotheaded in this scene, reinforcing all the characteristics we have come to associate with him throughout the play. Shakespeare conveys his arrogant nature through the statement, 'You shall find me apt enough to that, sir, an you will give me occasion'. This shows he is confident and ready to fight and also displays his provocative behaviour. He answers Mercutio's provoking statement with 'thou consortest with Romeo'. The word 'consortest' is used as an insult towards both Romeo and Mercutio, and suggests that they are both lower-class people.

The student continues her investigation of this scene. In her work here and elsewhere it is clear that she is able to sustain her interpretation of character and select appropriately. Her work is carefully rooted in the text, and ends:

Overall, Tybalt's portrayal throughout the play leads me to the conclusion that he is aggressive and motivated as much by his desire to fight as to uphold the family honour. Mercutio on the other hand is a more peaceful man, although he is perfectly happy to fight when necessary. He seems to be motivated not by a deep and resentful desire for blood but instead by a provocative and rather childish and flippant attitude to life. His death brings an end to the light-heartedness he brought to the play. Significantly, his final speech 'A plague on both your houses' ushers in the escalating tragedy.

This student has fulfilled the requirements of the Assessment Objectives. She has read and understood her material; she has made a selection of appropriate detail from the text to support her views; she has developed and sustained her interpretation of Shakespeare's ideas and perspectives.

To be successful in this part of the controlled assessment, students need to:
- be completely confident that they have understood the chosen text
- be able to select material appropriate for the particular task while keeping in mind that they need to refer to the entire text in their responses
- plan carefully
- be able to make close reference to text to support their points.

Advice for students

Finally, some advice for students before they tackle any of the Reading controlled assessment tasks:
- Know your texts as well as you can. You may take them into the assessment session for controlled assessment, but it is best not to rely on them. Just use them for reference.
- Do not waste your time on a lot of biographical detail at the beginning of an essay. It will not gain you marks and it will waste your time.
- Think carefully what the task is asking you to do and do it. Do not let your attention slip away from your task while you are writing.
- You are allowed to take one sheet of notes with you into the assessment session. These notes must not contain a plan or a draft, but you may wish to jot down key quotations or page references.
- Remember that you need to refer to the texts when you are writing. You will not get many marks if you simply state something without supporting it.
- The highest marks go to candidates who investigate how the writer has used the language to shape the reader/audience's feelings and views.
- Take care to write as accurately as possible, then your meaning will be clear.

Controlled assessment guidance
Open writing

Introduction

This section of the Teacher Guide provides you with guidance on the new controlled assessment element of the WJEC specification. It aims to familiarise you with the WJEC specification requirements for either GCSE English or GCSE English Language and help you to teach the controlled assessment tasks in Open/Creative writing.

Controlled assessment is compulsory for all students and is not tiered. Specific differentiation advice for Higher and Foundation students is included in this guidance.

Guidance

Specification requirements

AO4 Writing
* Write to communicate clearly, effectively and imaginatively, using and adapting forms and selecting vocabulary appropriate to task and purpose in ways which engage the reader
* Organise information and ideas into structured and sequenced sentences, paragraphs and whole texts, using a variety of linguistic and structural features to support cohesion and overall coherence
* Use a range of sentence structures for clarity, purpose and effect, with accurate punctuation and spelling

One third of the available credit is allocated to this last part of AO4.

The WJEC specification requires learners to write accurately and fluently:
* choosing content and adapting style and language to a wide range of forms, media, contexts, audiences and purposes
* adapting form to a wide range of styles and genres.

In the external assessment, students are required to write two pieces in response to transactional tasks. This aspect of the assessment tests the 'contexts, audiences and purposes' requirement.

In the Writing section of controlled assessment in GCSE English, students are required to write a piece of first-person writing and a piece of third-person writing.

In the Writing section of controlled assessment in GCSE English Language, students are required to write a description piece and a narrative/expressive piece.

'Controlled' implies that the students will attempt their work in controlled conditions with a strict time limit.

In both cases the mechanical aspects (SSPS) will be awarded a third of the marks available.

Since descriptive writing requires particular skills, it will be considered separately in this section of the Teacher Guide (see pages 130–133).

Limitations

Tasks

The generic tasks noted above will not change throughout the life of the WJEC Specification. Specific tasks will be provided by WJEC on an annual basis. The first tasks will be set in April 2010. After this, new specific tasks will be set each April.

Task-taking

During the teaching and learning stage, students may have access to resources and advice. Work may be written in draft form and teachers may advise students on approaches, but the work may not be marked closely for mechanical errors.

In the final assessment session, students are allowed 2 hours to complete the two pieces of work. It is not necessary for students to produce both Writing pieces at the same assessment session, as long as the complete time taken does not exceed the time limit of 2 hours.

Students are not allowed to take drafts into the final assessment session. Work may be word-processed, but students are not allowed access to dictionaries or spell-checker/grammar programs, or the internet or their personal school computer files.

If the assessment session is divided into shorter periods of time, all the students' work must be collected and stored safely.

Marking and external moderation

The work will be marked within the centre using the assessment criteria provided by WJEC (see page 8). Each piece will be marked out of 20 using the assessment criteria. Please see the specification for these criteria.

It will be expected that internal moderation will establish a rank order from which the sample will be chosen for the external moderator. All students and teachers will have to sign a coversheet as proof of authenticity. Details of tasks and marks will also be entered on this coversheet, which will accompany students' folders if they are sent to the external moderator.

All centres will receive a brief report on the work of the students and the standard of assessment.

Planning

Practical approaches

It would probably be sensible to consider the two pieces of writing required discretely rather than expecting students to complete both on the same occasion. Below is one possible approach to teaching this part of the course.

- Over a period of time, teach the skills for the chosen type of writing. Later in the Teacher Guide (pages 124–133), these skills are looked at in more detail.
- Students could then be given an opportunity to practise these skills either discretely or collectively. This work may be marked in the normal way.
- The specific tasks for the year could be introduced and possible approaches considered. It is important at this stage that individuality is not stifled by a 'group' approach.
- Arrange a time for the final assessment session. Students are allowed 2 hours in total and it is the centre's choice how this time is divided between the two writing pieces. If students are attempting the GCSE English Language qualification, it would seem sensible to think in terms of about 45 minutes for the description and 1 hour 15 minutes for the narrative/ expressive writing. If they are attempting the GCSE English Language qualification, then the time could be more equally split.
- The final assessment session may take place in the classroom or, perhaps more conveniently, in an examination hall where a larger number of students may be tested at once.
- It is important that students do not have notes with them in the final assessment session for the Writing assessment. If word-processors are used, ensure that grammar/spell-check programs are switched off and that students do not have access to the internet or their personal school files.
- If the assessment session spreads over more than one lesson, students' work must be collected and securely stored. They may not redraft work once the session is over.

- Make sure all students have signed a coversheet.
- Keep the work securely in readiness for the submission of the moderation sample.

Other notes:
- The work must be kept in the centre for 6 months after the examination results are published, in case of any appeals.
- After January 2012, students may submit a complete controlled assessment folder (including the necessary Reading content) in either January or June.

Writing: Open writing/Using language

Narrative and expressive writing

The WJEC GCSE English and English Language specifications expect two pieces of writing from each student. In the WJEC GCSE English Language controlled assessment structure, the requirements are one piece of descriptive and one piece of narrative/ expressive writing. The WJEC GCSE English controlled assessment folder requires one piece of first-person and one piece of third-person writing.

Clearly the descriptive writing considered below (pages 130–133) could be either first or third person. However, it requires particular skills which are slightly more refined than those for more general open writing such as indicated by the simple title 'narrative/expressive'.

It seems convenient, therefore, to consider all 'non-descriptive' types of writing as a group, since they are likely to have similar characteristics.

Teaching discrete skills

The tasks will be provided by WJEC exam board, but can be interpreted in any way the student feels is appropriate. They are designed to be as open as possible. In preparing students for this part of the course, teachers may like to consider the following aspects:
- plot and structure (first-person/autobiographical/ third-person)
- characterisation
- the establishment of atmosphere
- the use of dialogue
- selection of detail
- narrative hooks
- accuracy.

Plot and structure

Content

The most serious mistake a student can make regarding this aspect is to attempt to write a piece which is overcomplicated. The best advice is to keep the plot as simple as possible. For this reason some approaches do not work well. These include:

- Fantasy writing where it is necessary to create an alternative world. Necessarily this will take up rather too much of the available time allowance. This type of writing also often lacks credibility and will be event-driven, not allowing for the creation of believable characterisation and the establishment of relationships.
- 'Adventure' stories where the structure relies on complex plotting. Again in the time allowed, there is not the opportunity to develop relationships and feelings. Such writing generally relies on fast action. This type of writing is difficult for students to handle.
- Any type of writing that involves ghosts, the supernatural, walks in the woods and haunted houses. Generally speaking such experiences are outside the knowledge of the students, and are often based on films or computer games.

The best way for a student to avoid these pitfalls is to choose a topic which is simple and personal, preferably something of which he or she has some personal experience. For this reason autobiographical writing, for example, will generally be successful (see below) and will fit very well into the first-person piece in the GCSE English controlled assessment specification. Similarly in the GCSE English Language folder, students will be given at least one title which can be interpreted in an autobiographical way. However, this is not the only route to success and other approaches are considered below.

Approaches to creating a plot structure: first-person/autobiographical

Most students will probably wish to adopt a linear approach to plotting. This structure has many benefits. Characters can be established from the outset and they can be linked into personal feelings. The essential aspect of plot structuring is planning. Those who take an 'I'll work it out as I go along' approach, which is frequently an aspect of less able students' responses to open writing, will not create convincing narratives. One of the advantages of the controlled assessment structure is that students can be given time to plan what they wish to write about and how they want to shape their writing.

Examples of approaches to first-person or autobiographical writing

The first stage is to think of a central incident. This does not need to be particularly serious or important, though it may be. The essential aspect is that it is uncomplicated in detail and thus will allow the student to build up a structure around it that will involve the emotions of the readers without having to tell too much 'story'. The development of character is also easier if the central incident is simple.

Below is an example of a simple incident being built up into a full narrative. It is planned on the basis of:

- central incident
- the mood the writer wants to give the piece as a whole
- basic plan
- more detailed notes.

> **Central idea:** younger brother falling off his bike and lands in a rose bush.

At this stage the writer needs to think about the general mood he or she wants to create. This will be based on his or her attitude to the younger sibling.

> **Mood/attitude to incident:** serves him right/pride before a fall/writer finds the incident funny and enjoys the reactions of parents and enjoys the fact that the brother gets slightly hurt.

Once this idea has been established in the student's plan, details may be built around it.

> **Basic plan**
> - details of the event
> - character of brother
> - reaction of writer
> - reaction of parents
> - outcomes

Now this basic structure has been established, the student can start embellishing the details.

> **Extended plan**
>
> **Details of the event**
> - cul-de-sac setting
> - curving low wall into driveway of home
> - grass front lawn
> - brother's usual way of stopping/getting off the bike was to fall off on the grass
> - on this occasion missed the entry onto the grass and hit the wall, catapulting himself into the rose bush
> - tears and scratches
> - mum and dad watching and rush out to help him
> - no serious damage

Character of brother

- daredevil
- not able to use brakes on the bike
- too small to ride it
- in fact riding writer's bike rather than his own
- does not seem to care if he gets hurt
- no understanding of the risks

Reaction of writer

- knew it was going to happen
- pleased that his or her full-of-himself brother had come to grief
- writer realises how different he or she is from brother
- happy he or she does not make fool of him or herself – bit more grown up

Reaction of parents

- mum overprotective
- all for rushing brother to casualty despite the minor nature of injuries
- cradles brother in her arms to stop the screaming
- offers 'treats' to heal the wounds
- writer feels that he or she would not be treated in the same way – meant to be more grown up
- father finds the incident funny
- thinks it will teach the brother some sense

Outcome

- writer believes that brother once more gets all the attention when in fact he deserves to be hurt for being so stupid

Although this plan appears to be linear, there is no need for the student to deal with it in that way. He or she can mix the points up, introducing information when it is relevant.

It is also worth stressing that since the central incident is very simple, the focus of the story is on the writer's reactions to the incident. These will reveal character and feelings fully.

The next stage is to consider a strong opening to the piece. It needs to attract and hold the reader's attention and provide an entertaining lead-in to the incident. If possible, it is a good idea to suggest the writer's attitude immediately.

Suggested activity

The following possible openings could be considered with students.
- I remember the day my brother fell into a rose bush.
- It had to happen sooner or later – he was just asking to get hurt the way he rode that bike.
- When I was little we lived in a house with a curved wall leading into the drive.
- I have a younger brother who is always doing silly things.
- It was a lovely sunny day and my brother and I were playing in front of the house where we lived.

All of these openings are reasonable, but some invite the reader to ask questions, and this is what is likely to make him or her continue to read. Students could be invited to invent better openings for this story structure.

Suggested activity

Students could be asked to choose a similarly simple incident and plan a structure like the one above. They should be reminded that what happens is not as important as people's reaction to what happens.

This example of first-person or autobiographical writing is based on a relatively trivial incident. Some students find it easier to write about a serious matter, and often this involves the death of a loved one, typically a grandparent. Since such an event is likely to have left a deep impression on the student, it is relatively easy for him or her to write effectively on such a subject. The same approach to building a structure can be employed. Once again, because the central incident is simple, the student can concentrate on character, feelings and atmosphere.

If this topic is too sensitive for your class it could be changed for the death of a pet. Such topics often bring out the best in students, especially weaker ones.

Central idea: death of grandparent

Mood/attitude to incident: serious, sad, regretful, tearful, but happy in terms of memories

Basic plan
- realisation that something is wrong with grandparent
- hospital visits
- being told of the death
- reactions of relatives
- memories of better times

Extended plan

Realisation
- hushed conversations between parents/relatives – worry
- understanding that something serious is happening – fear

- visit to grandparent's home – changes in welcome – uncertainty in the air
- being told by parents that grandparent not well – hospital

Hospital visits
- atmosphere and reaction to going into hospital geriatric ward/perhaps contrast with when writer visited mother with newborn sibling in hospital
- paraphernalia of hospital ward – tubes, monitors – fear
- changed look of grandparent – loving concern
- despite grandparent's attempt to smile, writer deeply upset and realising that she is really ill/ contrast with happier times
- leaving hospital – regrets

Being told of death
- night phone call – realisation that the end is near
- hurried off to neighbour/relative in nightclothes – fear about the unusual situation
- parents drive off – sleeplessness
- neighbour/relative breaking the news
- sadness and tears

Memories of better times
- ending concerned with the good as well as (more recent) bad memories
- finish with how the writer wants to remember his or her grandparent

Approaches to creating a plot structure: third person

Writing a third-person narrative is probably a more difficult task, since the student is less likely to be working directly from memory. Again, the best approach is for the student to pick a relatively simple situation upon which he or she can build a convincing set of characters and emotions. As noted above, certain approaches do not help students to give of their best and are better avoided. Instead, they could choose human experiences on which to base their stories.

In both GCSE English and GCSE English Language, students will be given a choice of titles on which to base a third-person narrative. It is worth remembering that it is only in the GCSE English folder that there must be a third-person narrative. In the GCSE English Language folder, students could in theory write two first-person pieces, but as noted above, the required 'descriptive' writing is probably best attempted in the third person.

The tasks given will give some clue as to possible approaches and suitable situations. They will be very general and open to a number of interpretations, thus giving maximum freedom to the students.

As an example, students could be given a task like this:

Write a story in the third person about a situation where a relationship fails.

The first step is to make a list of possible relationships. For example:
- parent/child
- 'best' friends
- a love relationship
- working relationship.

Having chosen one of these or another not on this list, the student needs to plan the work. For example, if the student chose the 'best friends' option the plan could be constructed as follows:

Central idea: two girls/boys who have been friends since childhood are split because one steals the other's boy/girlfriend

Mood: happy in original relationship, moving to sense of betrayal, to sadness at what has been lost

Basic plan
- background to the relationship
- characters of the people involved
- the point where the relationship breaks and the reasons for it
- the aftermath

Extended plan

Background to the relationship
- first meeting
- things in common
- shared experiences that bind the two together

Characters of the two people involved
- one shy and retiring, not keen to take risks
- the other open and lively, always popular with other people
- the lead-in to the break-up
- the point where the relationship breaks
- the 'shy' character stealing the lively character's boy/girlfriend
- the actual occasion of discovery (crisis in the story)

The aftermath
- the break-up of the relationship – recriminations
- the final lines reflecting the mood – perhaps regretful, sad

It helps the student if he or she bases the characters on real people. This will make the emotional content easier to handle and more real. It will be noticed that in this scenario, virtually nothing happens apart from the central incident where the reason for the break-up becomes apparent. This focuses the student's mind on to the creation of credible characters and an investigation of what they are feeling.

With a topic like this, there is no need for a linear approach. The story can begin at any point in the narrative and this can provide the student with a dramatic opening which will draw the reader in to wanting to know more.

Suggested activity

Students could look at these openings to see which would entice them to read further into the story:

1 Andrea and Kate had been friends for as long as they could remember. They had shared everything from the day they met in nursery school.

2 This is a story about two girls called Kate and Andrea who had a row over a boyfriend.

3 Kate met Andrea on the corner as usual, but her friend looked troubled.

4 Kate was astounded by what she saw as she entered the room. Her so-called friend was in the arms of the man she loved.

5 That was the last time they met. Afterwards they both bitterly regretted the loss of their friendship over such a wimp.

It will be obvious that in the first and second openings, the student has started at the beginning of the story. In the third, the illicit relationship has clearly begun and so the student would need to do a little backtracking to explain the situation. The fourth hits right in on the central incident. Here the 'good' relationship between the girls could then be considered in the light of this betrayal, adding more depth to the story. This is also true of the last option, where the student begins at the end of the story. Looking with hindsight at the relationship allows plenty of opportunity to uncover the clues that lead to the deception. This approach is not possible if a linear approach is taken, and is more demanding in terms of plot construction.

When these different openings have been considered, students should begin to realise that there is more than one way of organising the structure once the basic plan has been established. They can begin the work at the beginning, at the point of crisis or at the end, making the piece reflective with the central character simply looking back on the occasion of the break-up.

Summing up

In terms of planning therefore, the process could be:

1 Decide on the basic interpretation of the title after looking at a number of options. This could be a classroom activity of the brainstorming type.

2 Decide on the mood, or moods, of the piece as a whole, bearing in mind that a good writer manipulates the reader's feelings.

3 Decide on the number of characters and relationship between them if this is not already dictated by the basic interpretation of the title.

4 Plan in more detail, listing the aspect that will come in each section of the story.

5 Decide at which point in the plan the story will 'begin'.

6 Consider very carefully the opening sentence to ensure that it involves and interests the reader.

7 When the story is finished, reconsider the final lines to ensure that they reflect the mood of the piece as a whole.

Suggested activity

Students could be asked to construct similar plans for the other failing relationships listed above. At all times, they should be encouraged to forget about action and think instead about reactions. Generally, it is how we react to other people that is interesting rather than the events which cause the reaction.

Characterisation

It is wise for the student to have only two or three characters in their story. If more people are introduced into the writing, the student loses the room to develop personality. The characters need to be considered 'in the round' rather than simply as physical specimens. Thus details about height, weight, etc. are often less interesting than the one physical characteristic which makes a person stand out. Students could be encouraged to see people 'in the round' rather than as two-dimensional. An emotional reaction to a character is always more interesting than the physical details.

Suggested activity

In preparation for the Open writing controlled assessment task, students could write brief character sketches of themselves or friends. The emphasis should be on what makes the person interesting rather than physical details.

In addition, students could analyse the following two examples of writing to see which is the more effective.

---

1 Jack had dark hair and was rather fat. He wore size ten shoes and was always in a suit. He always wore a tie and his shirts were crisp and white. He was a banker and liked to show off his wealth. He always drank champagne when he was out and he was kind enough to treat all his friends. He drove an expensive car and liked his holidays abroad skiing in the winter and sailing in the summer.

2 Across the room Mary spotted Dave. This was not difficult as he was about seven feet tall. That was what made him stand out – literally. At parties he would tower over the other teenagers as if he was searching for a basketball ring to drop a ball into, because that was where he really belonged. Some

American team should snap him up, though Mary doubted if he would score many baskets since under the height she knew he was as soft as butter. She had always liked him, even though, at 18 inches shorter, she had to look up to him like some kind of god. He was a gentle god, though, and she had never known him to say a cruel word to anybody. She moved in his direction.

Besides looking at the way these two characters have been described, students may also look at the sentence structures and vocabulary of the two pieces. Fairly obviously, the key issue is that the first remains superficial and we only learn about external features, because the writer is not thinking about his or her reaction to the person. In the second extract, the student has clearly thought about Mary's reactions as well as the aspects of Dave which make him different. Part of the success of this description relies on the contrast between the appearance and Dave himself, and that is made clear by the personal involvement.

It is good advice for students to try to paint details of a character in passing rather than setting out to give a full description before the narrative begins. In the second description, Mary spotting Dave across a room gives the description some setting and the description leads successfully into the dialogue that will follow.

Suggested activity

Students could be encouraged to write descriptions of characters within situations. For example:

- a headteacher walking into assembly in the morning
- a security officer walking around a supermarket
- a boy playing football with his friends
- a builder on a building site
- a shopworker serving a customer.

Establishing atmosphere

Establishing atmosphere is mostly about vocabulary choices. Flat and dull vocabulary will not suggest a sense of place in a story. Students should be encouraged to think about vocabulary choices before writing, since the words chosen inevitably colour the reader's perception of the event or scene.

Suggested activity

Students could look at the following two extracts and think about which creates the best sense of the atmosphere in the scene.

---

1 The fishing boats filled the harbour. Old men were working on their nets while holiday makers sat at tavernas and drank their cold drinks. A large white yacht pulled into the harbour and the harbourmaster rushed to take the ropes to tie it up. Otherwise nobody moved, apart from the stray cat that was always creeping around hoping for scraps from the tourists' tables. The heat was overwhelming. As midday approached, the shopkeepers began to close their doors and shutters, retiring for a siesta.

2 The bleak walls of the room reflected only the dull light that filtered through the filthy window. Slumped on the ramshackle and half collapsed bed, Jackie slowly tried to understand where she was and why she was there. Suddenly, the overhead light flashed on revealing the full awfulness of her prison, because she now realised, that is exactly what it was. The bright illumination only made her more terrified. The walls which had looked bleak now seemed much worse. They revealed that they were marked with cross-hatching and scoring which suggested that the previous occupant had spent many days in this hopeless situation.

The first piece attempts to suggest the fierce heat and slow pace of life in a Mediterranean harbour, but the vocabulary choices are weak. Students could rewrite the piece, improving the vocabulary so that the reader feels involved and interested in what is going on. The second piece has carefully chosen vocabulary to indicate the horror and filth of the place. Students could identify the vocabulary that creates this grim picture. Alternative words could be considered, or students could write a more cheerful passage where atmosphere is created by careful choice of vocabulary.

The use of dialogue

It is sensible for students to include a little dialogue in their narrative work. Not only does it display some punctuation skills, but it can also move the story on or be an interesting opening gambit.

However, there is the risk that the student will write far too much dialogue once they get started, and to use it successfully, students must be confident that they can lay it out in the correct way. It is probably better not to use it at all than to get the paragraphing and punctuation wrong.

As noted, it can be a useful way to begin a story, especially if the speech is dramatic. Dialogue can also be used in short snatches in the descriptive writing.

Suggested activity

Students could use speech to write dramatic openings to any of the tasks noted above.

Too often in students' work the dialogue becomes protracted and dull, especially when it is concerned with trivia. Students could compare these two examples of the use of dialogue in stories.

---

1 The wind was strong that day. Peter carefully took the baby Chloe out of her car seat and held the door open for the two boys to get out onto the drive. A sudden gust snatched the door from his hand.

'Dad!' screamed Jake as the blood began to flow from his fingers.

Still clutching the baby, his father looked with horror at his son's hand.

'Back in the car!' he shouted to the two boys as he restrapped Chloe into her seat.

The journey to casualty was punctuated with Jake's moans as he carefully cradled his injured hand, now wrapped in his dad's white handkerchief. Only it wasn't white any longer...

2 Jenny called up her friend Karen to arrange their evening.

'Hi, Karen. Fancy a night out?'

'Hey, why not? We seem to have done nothing but work this week,' her friend replied.

'Good, where shall we go?'

'Don't know. I must have some tea first. I'm starving.'

'I'll tell you what we'll do. You have some tea and give me a call when you've finished. I want a shower anyway.'

'Right oh. Mum's calling. Must go. Speak to you later.'

The first extract uses the dialogue sparingly and to great effect. The dialogue moves the action on and expresses the pain and urgency of the situation. In the second, the empty dialogue goes nowhere and does not enhance any aspect of the narrative. It also fails to develop character.

> **Suggested activity**
>
> Students could take a simple situation like arriving home from school or coming down for breakfast, and write an opening paragraph in which they use dialogue. They could be limited to one line, to focus their minds on making the speech important to the atmosphere and the establishment of character.

Selection of detail

Since students have a limited time to write their final pieces, it is important that they use detail economically. The very best will be able to see what is important to the atmosphere, characterisation, establishment of mood and interest of the reader. Those who are less careful will include all sorts of unnecessary detail which will result in the reader losing interest. The classic example of this inclusion of unnecessary detail is the 'I got out of bed and had a wash...' approach. On some occasions, getting out of bed may be important to the story as a whole, but this is not often the case.

> **Suggested activity**
>
> Students could write a third-person piece based on this task:
> **Write a story in the third person about a situation where a relationship fails.**

Both decided to set the scene in a school playground where a boy and girl, who had been going out together, split up.

1 John hurried to the playground passing the different classrooms and looking into each as he walked down the corridor. There were lots of children playing football on the field and he saw his mates in a particularly vigorous game. He took off his sweatshirt and joined in. Then he saw Jess coming across towards him. 'I'll be back in a minute,' he shouted to his friends and walked towards Jess, avoiding a football as it came hurtling towards him. The sun glinted off the wet plastic as it passed him. Jess arrived and he asked her why she had dumped him. The school bell began to ring and the children began to file into school. John thought he had better hurry this up or he would be late for registration.

'I don't like you any more after I saw you with Angie. You cheated on me,' was all she said. He turned and walked away.

2 John watched the footballs being kicked about by the younger boys as he waited for Jess to stroll over to him. There was no urgency in the way she walked and it was as if she was wandering to Science, a lesson he knew she hated. She greeted him in a half-hearted fashion, pushing her hair away from her eyes. Nothing in her expression suggested that she was in the least interested in what he had to say.

'So, what's the problem?' she asked, her eyes wandering towards the younger boys.

John resisted the temptation to snap at her that she was the problem – her lack of interest, the dismissive way she had abruptly ended their telephone conversation the previous night, the cruel little email she had sent ending their relationship.

'I want to know why you dumped me,' he at last muttered, trying all the time to will her eyes to look at him again.

When she did, it was with anger. 'It may have something to with seeing you with Angie last week,' she hurled at him.

The first piece is full of unnecessary detail which submerges the central issue almost completely. Students could be asked to strip out all the information that is not essential. The second example is well-focused and concentrates fully on the break-up of the relationship. The student adds details that support his picture and make it more credible. Students could analyse the detail to see how it all fits together.

Narrative hooks

If the narrative has been carefully planned, students may wish to use 'narrative hooks' to draw the reader in and suggest future developments. Necessarily these will occur early in the essay and are often associated with a reflective opening. For example, this student began an essay on a disturbing or traumatic event with the following:

It happened a while ago. Everyone had forgotten. Chris hadn't. It was impossible when it was all she dreamed about and everything she did drew her back to that fateful day.

The rest of the essay led to the 'fateful' day. Similar narrative hooks can be seen in some of the essay openings noted above.

Accuracy

A third of the marks are given to this aspect and since students will not be able to refer to dictionaries and thesauri, they will be going into the final assessment session with only their own skills and expertise to support them. Word-processors may be used, but any spelling- and grammar-checking programs must be disenabled and students must not have access to the internet or their personal school computer files.

Accuracy is, therefore, very important. As teachers are sure to be aware, the main issues are:

- comma splicing
- omission of apostrophes (both elision and possessive)
- the misplacing of apostrophes
- direct speech punctuation and paragraphing
- misspelling of simple words, particularly homophones
- omission of paragraph demarcation
- uncertainty in subject/verb agreement
- inconsistency in tenses.

All teachers will have their own tried and tested ways of dealing with these issues. The most important point is to stress to students that if their technical accuracy is deficient, they will struggle to gain a C grade. It may be helpful for them to see a copy of the assessment criteria for the SSPS aspect of the assessment, and to grade their own work against the various mark bands. They could also be encouraged to 'mark' each other's work, since peer-assessment does tend to sharpen their focus on getting these aspects correct.

For more able students who are aiming for a high grade, simple technical accuracy is not likely to be a problem, but they should be aware that to gain high marks for this part of the course they need to be varying their sentence structures and using more sophisticated vocabulary and punctuation.

Advice to students

- Plan carefully – think about interesting details to include.
- Be realistic.
- Be careful that you don't write sentences without verbs.
- Zoom in rather than be general.
- Don't tell a story.
- Use the third person rather than the first.
- Choose your vocabulary carefully.
- Try to link up your details to give your work shape and cohesion.

Descriptive writing

Teaching discrete skills

Initial approaches

Students need to be aware of the issues relating to descriptive writing and how to succeed in the assessment session. One way of approaching this aspect of their course is to start with exemplar material, perhaps with some marginal notes to indicate qualities.

Before starting, students should be encouraged to note down the various aspects that could come in a description of the particular topic.

In descriptive writing the skills the students need to display to gain high marks are as follows:

Content and organisation

- 'zooming' and avoiding generalisation
- avoiding telling a story
- engaging the reader with entertaining detail
- using a variety of vocabulary suitable to the task
- being realistic
- avoiding verbless sentences
- linking up the descriptive details into a coherent whole.

Sentence structure, punctuation and spelling

- punctuate and spell accurately
- be consistent in tenses and agreements
- use paragraphs appropriately.

Below are examples of student work with examiner comments and grades, which should prove useful in your teaching. We have not given a mark or student exemplars for SSPS in these examples.

Zooming in and generalisation

Vague descriptions will not gain high marks. This student was asked to write a description of a busy railway or airport terminal.

The crowds were milling around the departure board searching for their platform numbers. Children were running around and demanding ice cream and sweets from their parents. Bored station cleaners leant on their brooms and stared at the clock looking forward to their next break. Smart office workers rushed to their platforms knowing exactly where they were going.

For the content and organisation aspect of the mark, this student would gain a C grade. He has chosen the right kinds of aspects to consider in his description and his vocabulary choices are good, but he has rushed his points and failed to 'zoom in'. Each of his sentences could be developed into a paragraph. He has generalised in his approach rather than picking out individuals. If he had taken a different approach, developing each of his points, the work would have gained a much higher mark. For example, his first sentence could be developed in this way:

A confused old lady stares at the departure board in the hope of finding her train listed. Struggling to focus on the mass of numbers, she changes her glasses and squints at the huge lettering above her head. Not finding the information she wants, she searches in vain around the station for a railway employee whom she could ask for help. Turning to her right she sees an equally confused couple and she appeals to them for information.

This work, if continued at this standard, would gain at least an A grade.

> **Suggested activity**
>
> Students could be asked to take the other sentences in the example above and expand them in a similar fashion.

Avoiding telling a story (often the result of choosing to write in the first person)

Weaker students often make this type of error. While it is not wrong to write in the first person, if this approach is adopted the result will often be narrative-based. Typically such accounts start long before the student actually reaches the place being described. This student, for example, was asked to describe a busy supermarket.

When I woke up mum was screaming at me to get out of bed and go with her to the supermarket. I turned over and tried to go back to sleep but she came up and pulled open my curtains and pulled off my duvet. I struggled downstairs and grabbed a piece of toast before mum dragged me to the car pushing shopping bags onto my lap. The trip to the supermarket was silent. I was still cross about being woken up and I couldn't understand why I had to go in the first place.

While this writing is quite engaging in its own way, it fails to fulfil the descriptive requirement, since the student has begun her work with a lengthy preamble. For content and organisation it would gain an E grade. She reaches the supermarket in the next paragraph, but by this time the moderator will have realised that the basic requirements of the task have not been met.

> **Suggested activity**
>
> Students could be asked to plan a description of a busy supermarket, being encouraged to make all their points clearly within the building and detailed.

Engaging the reader with entertaining detail

Descriptions rely on detail to give them life. If the student fails to include such detail, the work can become lifeless and 'flat'. A pedestrian approach will not gain high marks. This student was asked to write about being stuck in a traffic jam.

Looking out of the window I could see a workman holding a shovel. On the other side there was a line of cars and all the drivers were looking fed up. In the seat in front of me, the children were reading comics and didn't seem to realise that we had stopped. The bus driver was eating a sandwich while waiting for the traffic to clear.

While this student has made some attempt to 'zoom in', the details are rather flat and undeveloped. Each sentence could contain far more detail to develop the points. As it stands the description reads like a police report of the various activities. For content and organisation it would just gain a C grade.

> **Suggested activity**
>
> Students could be asked to take each sentence of the answer above and add interesting detail.

Using appropriate and interesting vocabulary

Good descriptive writing relies on appropriate and interesting vocabulary choices. Students need to be encouraged to think of the most appropriate words to convey the overall impression they want to make. To make a good impression, they need to go beyond the obvious vocabulary choices without trying to be too clever. While some students will rely on a very basic series of vocabulary choices, others will try to be too sophisticated in the language they choose. Both approaches will reduce the marks. Something between these two extremes is required for effective descriptive writing.

This student was asked to write a description of school sports day.

The day was sunny and bright and all the children ran around looking for their mums and dads. The race track was marked out on the field with white lines and the teachers all had whistles around their necks. The dads' race was starting and all the men tried to win to make their sons and daughters proud. One man stumbled and fell, causing others to trip over him, and soon there was a big pile of fathers on the field.

In this example the vocabulary is very simple indeed and the student has made no effort to engage the reader with words that would bring life to the piece. The opening is particularly 'flat' and almost clichéd, and a large number of students are likely to begin a description of this scene with variations upon the words 'day', 'sunny' and 'bright'. This example, if continued at this standard, would gain a D grade for content and organisation.

Suggested activity

Students could be asked to rewrite the example above, using a wider vocabulary and improving the interest level.

Being realistic

One of the dangers in descriptive writing is that the student is tempted to make the description too 'exciting'. Such students tend to believe that to engage and entertain the reader it is necessary to include great drama, particularly violence. It is important that students understand that the work needs to be based on real life. Including aspects that one would not normally come across in the chosen place can also lead the student towards a narrative approach.

This student was asked to write about a queue in the local post office.

Suddenly the doors swung open and in rushed three armed men. They pushed aside the customers in their rush to get to the tills. Everybody dropped to the floor when the first man waved his gun in the air. Nobody moved as the men demanded the contents of the till. Suddenly the shutters in front of the tills slammed down and the men were left looking at a wall of steel.

If the student had been asked to write about a raid on a post office, this would be a reasonable approach. However, the task asked him to describe the queue. The trick with this type of description, where experiences are likely to be similar for all students, is to look at what is ordinary and make it interesting for the reader. This will be achieved by looking in detail at the various characters. This work, if continued in the same way, would gain a D grade for content and organisation.

Suggested activity

Students could be asked to write interesting sentences or paragraphs on the following:
- a pensioner fussing about buying a couple of stamps
- a customer having a chat with the post office worker and holding everybody up
- a frazzled young mother with a screaming child.

To avoid the verbless sentence

This is one of the most common errors. When writing descriptively, students get absorbed by the requirement for detail and forget their understanding of sentence structure. The inability to write in complete sentences in this part of the assessment will inevitably result in a low mark. It will pay dividends if this weakness is identified early and corrected before bad habits are formed. Once students can recognise the verbless sentence, they will avoid the error. Generally the fault lies in students mistaking a present participle for a finite verb, as in the following example.

This student was asked to write a description of a park in summer.

Children running all over the place. Old men sitting on the park benches. The park keeper shouting at boys playing football on the grass. Ducks waddling to the pond. Toddlers being pushed on the swings by their mothers. Fathers sitting reading the newspaper.

Generally this problem can be solved by the inclusion of 'was' or 'were'. Even then the writing is rather lifeless and the sentence structures repetitive. Marks are awarded for sentence structures and students need to try to vary the way in which the sentences are opened. This example, if continued in the same way, would gain a D grade at most for content and organisation.

Suggested activity

Students could rewrite the example above, ensuring that they complete all the verbless sentences. As suggested above, this would still result in some rather dull writing. As a second task, they could make the description livelier by completely rewriting it.

Linking descriptive detail into a coherent whole

Another problem students encounter when writing descriptions is that they can write quite good descriptive detail but it lacks a sense of 'wholeness'. In other words, the writing becomes rather fragmented. This weakness is difficult to exemplify without reproducing a complete answer, but one way it can be avoided is for students to try to link paragraphs or ideas by making a connection between them. For example, in the middle of this student's description on a winter scene in a park, he wrote a description of the leafless trees, finishing it with:

...the trees had shed their leaves and they lay around the trunks in untidy heaps. A happy toddler tried to kick them high in the air, making his indulgent father smile...

This led on to a description of the toddler and father. One other route is to see the scene in a circular way, starting with a detail and working back to it at the end. Alternatively, able students can sometimes manage to use an extended metaphor throughout the entire piece.

> **Suggested activity**
>
> Students could be asked to take a complete descriptive piece that they have written, divide it up into its constituent parts and write linking sentences.

Mark scheme for sample Reading and Writing papers

Look at the first part of the newspaper article by Joanna Walters on page 171 of the Student Book.

Question 1: What do you learn from this part of the article about the inmates of Lakeview Shock Prison and the way they are treated? (10 marks)

0 marks: nothing attempted or fails to engage with the text and/or the question.

Give 1 mark for simple comments with occasional reference to the text, or unselective copying.

Give 2–4 marks (grades E/D), according to quality, for simple comments based on surface features of the text and/or awareness of more obvious implicit meanings.

Give 5–7 marks (grades C/B), according to quality, for valid, sensible comments based on a range of appropriate evidence from the text.

Give 8–10 marks (grades A/A*), according to quality, for a detailed and well-considered interpretation based on analysis and exploration of the text. These answers should show coherence and insight.

Some points:

- There are men and women prisoners
- They have to do 'army-style' physical training
- They are supervised by drill instructors
- They are regimented (chanting in unison)
- They have to show respect ('SIR')
- They are deprived of individuality (they wear 'regulation' clothes and are 'crop-headed')
- They are not violent but are 'a menace to society'
- They get compulsory education and drug treatment as well as military discipline
- Some are first offenders
- They choose the Shock programme and get released in six months
- They get up early and follow a strict programme of activities (plenty of examples)
- They get no days off
- The regime is 'spartan' (no television, magazines or recreation).

Overview:
- They are treated with military-style discipline
- They have to conform/do as they are told
- They are also given rehabilitation
- They are criminals who could become serious offenders.

Reward valid alternatives.

Now look at the rest of the article by Joanna Walters on page 172 of the Student Book.

Question 2: What impressions does Joanna Walters give of Sean Clarke and Eric Flowers? (10 marks)

0 marks: nothing attempted or fails to engage with the text and/or the question.

Give 1 mark for simple comments with occasional reference to the text, or unselective copying. These answers will struggle to engage with the text and/or the question.

Give 2–4 marks (grades E/D), according to quality, for simple comments based on surface features of the text and/or awareness of more straightforward implicit meaning.

Give 5–7 marks (grades C/B), according to quality, for appropriate detail from the text, showing understanding of the situation. These answers should be making inferences. Better answers should sustain a valid interpretation.

Give 8–10 marks (grades A/A*), according to quality, for appropriate detail from the text, explored with depth and insight. These answers should be thorough as well as perceptive, covering a range of points accurately and with an assured grasp.

Some points:
- He admits he was selfish and needed prison 'a long time ago'
- She gives details of his crimes (burglary, drugs and binge drinking)
- He admits he had no interest in change but 'learnt a lot' about himself
- He still has the tattoos but is now 'lean and healthy'
- He has a neat haircut and is smartly dressed
- He is looking forward to freedom but also a 'new life of integrity'
- He admits that he was a 'know-all' and got into a fight
- Clarke admits that he started getting into trouble when he was very young
- He was with 'a bad lot'
- Solitary confinement made him 'change my tune'
- They both have jobs lined up
- Flowers was a thief but now feels 'ashamed' of himself
- He admits he was 'horrible'
- He claims he has learnt to keep quiet and do as he is told

Overview:
- The writer gives details about the men to show the contrast between 'now and then'(they were tough, aggressive, criminals who have changed)
- Clarke has changed but Flowers has perhaps just learnt to keep out of trouble.

Reward valid alternatives.

Now look at the article 'Prison Boot Camps Prove No Sure Cure' on page 173 of the Student Book.

Question 3: How does this text try to show that the boot camp prison is 'no sure cure'? (10 marks)

0 marks: nothing attempted or fails to engage with the text and/or the question.

Give 1 mark for simple comments with occasional reference to the text, or unselective copying.

Give 2–4 marks (grades E/D), according to quality, for simple comments based on surface features of the text and/or awareness of more obvious implicit meanings/ persuasive techniques.

Give 5–7 marks (grades C/B), according to quality, for valid comments/inferences based on appropriate detail from the text. These answers should be addressing the issue of 'how', although they may rely on some spotting of key words or quotations. Better answers will have a clear focus on persuasive technique.

Give 8–10 marks (grades A/A*), according to quality, for a detailed exploration of the text and valid comments/ inferences. These answers should combine specific detail with overview and be fully engaged with analysis of persuasive technique.

'How' is partly a matter of content/presentation and partly a matter of language/structure. Look for a clear sense of 'how' as opposed to simply 'what'. The best answers take the extra step to analyse the detail rather than spotting it.

Some points:
- 'No one complained' at the early start and physical training in cold, wet weather
- The camp is described as 'gruelling'
- The inmates speak 'uneasily' about going home (not sure they can stay out of trouble)
- Mr Cooper is 'excited' but 'scared'
- He does admit he has to do it on his own and grow up so he is trying
- The statistics suggest that he is no more likely to stay out of trouble than 'normal' criminals
- It includes drug treatment and 'clean living' in the programme
- Inmates are monitored after release
- It is considered 'one of the best'

- There is education and therapy as well as hard labour and 'army-style' training
- It is not as successful as was hoped (high drop-out rate)
- Boot camp graduates do better at first, but reoffending is 'roughly the same' over four years
- Defenders say 'expectations were too high'
- It is not 'a quick fix' to serious social problems
- It *has* saved money and reduced overcrowding.

Overview:
- The evidence is mixed, so it is 'no sure cure' but not a total failure
- Uses statistics to show that success is not certain
- Uses interviews/examples/personal experience of inmates.

Reward valid alternatives.

Question 4: Compare and contrast what these two texts say about Lakeview Shock Prison. (10 marks)

To answer this question you will need to look at both texts. You should organise your answer into two paragraphs, using the following headings:
- the advantages of the 'shock' system
- the effect of the 'shock' system on the inmates.

0 marks: nothing attempted or fails to engage with the question and/or the text.

Give 1 mark for simple comments with occasional reference to the texts, or unselective copying.

Give 2–4 marks (grades E/D), according to quality, for simple comments based on surface features of the texts and/or awareness of more straightforward implicit meanings. Weaker answers could be a jumble of detail. Better answers should make some clear, if obvious, comparisons and contrasts.

Give 5–7 marks (grades C/B), according to quality, for valid comments/inferences based on appropriate detail from the texts. Better answers will show the ability to cross-reference in an organised way.

Give 8–10 marks (grades A/A*), according to quality, for valid comments/inferences based on a thorough and organised selection of appropriate detail from the texts. These answers should be coherent and insightful, ranging confidently across both texts.

Some points:
The advantages of the 'shock' system

Walters's article:
- It is 'highly effective'
- It provides education and drug treatment
- It 'shakes up' criminals
- It turns 'hoodlums' into 'keen workers'.

'No Sure Cure' article:

- Cooper seems willing to try to reform and stay out of trouble
- The system provides education, therapy and drug treatment
- It provides 'monitoring' after release
- It saves money
- It reduces overcrowding.

The effect of the 'shock' system on the inmates

Walters's article:

- They are disciplined and regimented
- It deprives them of individuality
- It motivates inmates
- It changes them for the better (examples of Clarke and Flowers).

'No Sure Cure' article:

- It makes them disciplined and compliant
- It seems to change them at first
- They are uneasy about release
- They are quite likely to re-offend
- A lot of them drop out.

Reward valid alternatives.

Content and organisation (13 marks)

Band 1   **1–3 marks**

- basic awareness of the purpose and format of the task
- some awareness of the reader/intended audience
- some relevant content despite uneven coverage of the topic
- simple sequencing of ideas provides some coherence
- paragraphs may be used to show obvious divisions or group ideas into some order
- some attempt to adapt style to purpose/audience (e.g. degree of formality)
- there is a limited range of vocabulary with little variation of word choice for meaning or effect

Band 2   **4–6 marks**

- shows awareness of the purpose and format of the task
- shows awareness of the reader/intended audience
- a sense of purpose shown in content coverage and some reasons are given in support of opinions and ideas
- sequencing of ideas provides coherence
- paragraphs are logically ordered and sequenced (e.g. topic sentences are supported by relevant detail)
- a clear attempt to adapt style to purpose/audience
- there is a some range of vocabulary, occasionally selected to convey precise meaning or to create effect

Band 3   **7–9 marks**

- shows clear understanding of the purpose and format of the task
- shows clear awareness of the reader/intended audience
- clear sense of purpose shown in content coverage; appropriate reasons given in support of opinions/idea
- ideas are shaped into coherent arguments
- paragraphs are used consciously to structure the writing
- style is adapted to purpose/audience
- there is a range of vocabulary selected to convey precise meaning or to create effect

Band 4   **10–13 marks**

- shows sophisticated understanding of the purpose and format of the task
- shows sustained awareness of the reader/intended audience
- content coverage is well-judged, detailed, and pertinent
- arguments are convincingly developed and supported by relevant detail
- ideas are selected and prioritised to construct sophisticated argument
- paragraphs are effectively varied in length and structure to control progression
- confident and sophisticated use of a range of stylistic devices adapted to purpose/audience
- a wide range of appropriate, ambitious vocabulary is used to create effect or convey precise meaning.

Sentence structure, punctuation and spelling (7 marks)

Band 1   1 mark

- sentences are mostly simple or compound
- compound sentences are linked or sequenced by conjunctions such as 'and' or 'so'
- punctuation (full stops, commas, capital letter to demarcate sentences) is attempted where appropriate and with some accuracy
- the spelling of simple words is usually accurate
- control of tense and agreement is uneven

Band 2   2–3 marks

- sentences are varied and both compound and complex sentences are used
- there is use of some subordination to achieve clarity and economy
- some control of a range of punctuation, including the punctuation of direct speech
- the spelling of simple and polysyllabic words is usually accurate
- control of tense and agreement is generally secure

Band 3   4–5 marks

- a range of grammatical structures is used to vary the length and focus of sentences
- simple, compound and complex sentences are used to achieve particular effects
- a range of punctuation is used accurately to structure sentences and texts, sometimes to create deliberate effects, including parenthetic commas
- most spelling, including that of irregular words, is usually correct
- control of tense and agreement is secure

Band 4   6–7 marks

- there is appropriate and effective variation of sentence structures
- there is a sophisticated use of simple, compound and complex sentences to achieve particular effects
- accurate punctuation is used to vary pace, clarify meaning, avoid ambiguity and create deliberate effects
- virtually all spelling, including that of complex irregular words, is correct
- tense changes are used confidently and purposefully

Additional task-specific guidance

Good answers may include some of the following features:

- a sustained sense of register and purpose which meets the requirement for a talk (for example, a lively, opinionated or witty approach)
- a clear and coherent approach (perhaps looking in details at one aspect of the topic or ranging more widely)
- a logical structure within which any argument is pursued effectively and clearly
- an evident sense of cohesion with material linked effectively (use of connectives/subordination)
- a range of appropriate and well-selected details to illustrate and give substance to ideas and opinions (skilful use of facts/figures/anecdotes)
- some development of ideas and opinions (perhaps involving alternative views)
- positioning and establishing a relationship with the reader via devices such as asides, questions, humour, use of active or passive voice and clear sense of audience
- ability to move from the general to the particular or vice–versa (specific examples used within a coherent approach to the topic)

Less successful answers may be characterised by some of the following features:

- uncertain sense of purpose and register (for example, ignoring the requirement for a talk)
- less secure control of structure (uncertain or random sequencing/no clear sense of argument)
- a tendency for details to be handled in isolation with limited sense of linking or cohesion (uneasy with connectives/subordination)
- details are thin or generalised with little sense of development (for example, a single sentence for each topic such as *everyone likes mobile phones*)
- limited development of ideas/opinions and a tendency to simple assertion (for example, *not having a mobile phone is ridiculous*)
- very limited awareness of the audience
- a tendency for comments to stay at the level of the 'general' and to lack specific examples

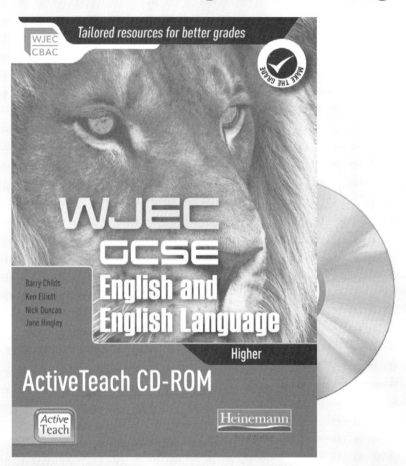